Lady Midrash

Lady Midrash

Poems Reclaiming the Voices of Biblical Women

Elisabeth Mehl Greene

Foreword by Kendra Weddle Irons

RESOURCE *Publications* · Eugene, Oregon

LADY MIDRASH
Poems Reclaiming the Voices of Biblical Women

Copyright © 2016 Elisabeth Mehl Greene. All rights reserved. Except for brief quotations in critical publications or reviews, no part of this book may be reproduced in any manner without prior written permission from the publisher. Write: Permissions, Wipf and Stock Publishers, 199 W. 8th Ave., Suite 3, Eugene, OR 97401.

Resource Publications
An Imprint of Wipf and Stock Publishers
199 W. 8th Ave., Suite 3
Eugene, OR 97401

www.wipfandstock.com

PAPERBACK ISBN: 978-1-4982-8419-6
HARDCOVER ISBN: 978-1-4982-8421-9
EBOOK ISBN: 978-1-4982-8420-2

Manufactured in the U.S.A.   06/02/2016

Scripture quotations marked (ESV) are from The Holy Bible, English Standard Version® (ESV®), copyright © 2001 by Crossway, a publishing ministry of Good News Publishers. Used by permission. All rights reserved.

Scripture quotations marked (NASB) are taken from the New American Standard Bible®, Copyright © 1960, 1962, 1963, 1968, 1971, 1972, 1973, 1975, 1977, 1995 by The Lockman Foundation. Used by permission. (www.Lockman.org)

Scripture quotations marked (NIV) are taken from the Holy Bible, New International Version®, NIV®. Copyright © 1973, 1978, 1984, 2011 by Biblica, Inc.™ Used by permission of Zondervan. All rights reserved worldwide. www.zondervan.com The "NIV" and "New International Version" are trademarks registered in the United States Patent and Trademark Office by Biblica, Inc.™

Scripture quotations marked (NKJV) are taken from the New King James Version®. Copyright © 1982 by Thomas Nelson. Used by permission. All rights reserved.

Cover art:
Flames: Photography by NOAA Photo Library, used with permission from Creative Commons Attribution 2.0; Apple: Photo by Jamie Mehl, used with permission; Rose: Photo by Elisabeth Mehl Greene; All others from the public domain.

To all the students of Lady Wisdom:
you writers,
you poets,
you scholars,
you researchers,
makers of music,
and askers of questions

Does not Story call out?

        Does not Midrash raise her voice?

                —after Proverbs 8:1

Contents

Foreword by Kendra Weddle Irons | xi
Acknowledgments | xiii
Introduction | xv

Part I: Tanakh

Eve *(The first woman)* | 3
Raouda *(Ruth)* | 5
Vashti *(Queen of Persia)* | 6
Nebiyah *(The prophetess who bore Isaiah's children)* | 8
Hajar *(Hagar)* | 10
Ya'el *(Destroyer of Sisera)* | 12
Jezebel *(Queen of Israel)* | 13
Jephthah's Daughter *(The sacrifice)* | 16
Rahab *(A woman of Jericho)* | 18
She'erah *(The builder)* | 21
Shulamith *(The beloved of Solomon)* | 22
Miriam *(The prophetess)* | 23
Saffūrah *(Zipporah)* | 24
Khuldah *(Huldah)* | 26
Dabourah *(Deborah)* | 28
Hannah *(The mother of Samuel)* | 29
Malikah *(Queen of Sheba)* | 31
Bathsheba *(The mother of Solomon)* | 33
Sahrai *(Sarah)* | 35
Rebeqah *(Rebecca)* | 37
Rahela *(Rachel)* | 39
Joseph *(The first child of Jacob and Rachel)* | 41
Shekinah *(God)* | 43

Noadiah *(The prophetess)* | 45
Irit *(The wife of Lot)* | 46
Yidana *(The witch of Endor)* | 49
Tamar *(The three)* | 51
Delilah *(The beloved of Samson)* | 53
Peninnah *(Wife of Elkanah)* | 55
Women of the Decalogue *(Women at Sinai)* | 57
Serakh bat Asher *(Daughter of Jacob's son Asher)* | 59

Part II: New Testament
Kalima *(The Syro-Phoenician woman)* | 63
Shahar *(The woman accused of adultery)* | 65
Maryam an-Nasiri *(Mary, mother of Jesus)* | 67
Anna *(The prophetess)* | 69
Salome *(The dancer)* | 71
Junia *(The apostle)* | 73
Samara *(The Samaritan woman)* | 74
Philip's Daughters *(Four women who prophesied)* | 76
Nuntia *(The wife of Pilate)* | 77
The Maji *(Wise travelers from the East)* | 79
Niyyah *(The woman with the alabaster jar)* | 81
Sapphira *(The woman accused of fraud)* | 83
Joanna *(Wife of Herod's chief of staff)* | 84
Shoshan *(Susanna)* | 85
Damaris *(An Athenian)* | 86
Rhoda *(A slave)* | 88
Tabitha *(A disciple)* | 89
Laishah & Eunike *(The grandmother and mother of Timothy)* | 90
Mariam al-Majdal *(Mary Magdalene)* | 91
Prisca *(Priscilla)* | 92
Phoebe *(A deacon)* | 93
Ilisabaʻ *(Elizabeth)* | 94
Candace *(Queen of Ethiopia)* | 96
Bracha *(The woman who blessed the mother of Jesus)* | 99

The "Other" Mary *(One of many)* | 100
Kyria *(Beloved lady of Second John)* | 102
Martha *(Sister of Mary and Lazarus)* | 103
Tryphaena & Tryphosa *(God's workers)* | 104
Lysia *(A sister of Jesus)* | 105
Chloe *(A leader of the church in Corinth)* | 106

Abbreviations | 109
End Notes | 111

Foreword

People often admit—secretly, of course—they find Bible-reading boring. This is because they have lost the indispensable gift of imagination. Taught to read without this important skill, it is no surprise the Bible, for all of its apparent popularity, is actually seldom read by the very people who claim it to be a holy text.

In my approximately fifteen years of teaching introductory Bible courses to university students, the most important interpretive approach I've tried to teach is the one Elisabeth Mehl Greene so astutely illustrates with this remarkable collection of poems: informed imagination. Midrash, the ancient Jewish practice of asking *what if?*, begins by utilizing one's imagination to ask questions of the Bible that usually are not considered.

Such questions form the foundation of *Lady Midrash: Poems Reclaiming the Voices of Biblical Women*. In these smart and perceptive poems, Greene takes her readers on a pilgrimage of a lifetime, one that will liberate the Bible from its dusty—and holy—perch to an inspired space of godly interrogation. Within these pages expect to be swept up into the power of questions and paradoxes, of contradictions and quandaries.

For some, such intentional probing misrepresents the Bible. It is much safer to believe God never changes and therefore the Bible reflects a similar inflexibility.

But such intransigence fails to take seriously the teaching method Jesus used. His parables with their twists and turns never provided easy or tidy answers, but always required sustained reflection and a willingness to be surprised and disarmed. Being neighborly means transgressing religious law to help a stranger who is also one's enemy? A woman who searches for her lost coin is an image of God? What?!

Similarly, midrash requires active listening so that questions rather than statements are cultivated and considered.

In *Lady Midrash*, Greene uses sound scholarship, attentiveness to details, creativity, and imagination to listen to women who are in the Bible but who have mostly been lost to us. This is accomplished in a number of effective ways from changing or providing new names, to bringing focus to

Foreword

cultural identity, to shifting the attention from male autonomy to female actor. The result is that women who usually are unnamed, unexplored, or even erased, are brought to our awareness so that we might hear their voices, might consider what they would have told us if they had been given a chance.

Hagar (Hajar), for example, conveys how easily she was overlooked, her immigrant status rendering her invisible. And yet, despite how she was treated by others, God noticed her sorrow. Subsequently, Hajar, while in the desert, named God (an interesting contrast to Moses' experience of being told God's name).

Or consider Jephthah's daughter, an unnamed woman whose help did not come from the hills. In *Lady Midrash* we are confronted by her plight; we must notice the inconsistency embedded in our holy writ. Neither Isaac nor Ishmael were sacrificed. But Jephthah's daughter—unnamed, "just a girl"—was dispensable. What does this suggest about God?

Several of these poems invite recognition of absurdities. "Women of the Decalogue" and "Junia," for example, show the potential of understanding God as separate from the religious systems that develop over time and therefore reflect society's misogyny. Too, "Kalima," in her tenacious argument with Jesus, leaves nothing left unsaid, catapulting us out of our lazy assumptions about his humanity.

Readers will want to absorb this book, returning to it multiple times. Considered closely and deeply, it will change how people approach the Bible. *Lady Midrash* displays Elisabeth Mehl Greene's insightful and creative work so well it will make reading the Bible exciting—and challenging, a combination that will keep those Bibles dust-free!

Kendra Weddle Irons, Ph.D.
Associate Professor of Religion and Humanities,
Texas Wesleyan University
Co-Author of *If Eve Only Knew: Freeing Yourself from Biblical Womanhood & Becoming All God Means for You to Be* (Chalice Press, 2015)
Irving, Texas

Acknowledgments

Thanks to:

Wipf and Stock Publishers for believing in *Lady Midrash*.

The Prince Alwaleed bin Talal Center for Muslim-Christian Understanding at Georgetown University for facilitating the research that went into this project.

Zinah Kareem, the Middle East Institute in Washington D.C., and the city of Abu Dhabi for starting me on my Arabic language learning journey.

Language experts Sarah Baker, Kyle Biersdorff, and Dania Thafer for advice regarding matters of Biblical and regional languages.

Manuscript readers and poetry listeners, Jessica Abbazio, Nick Carpenter, Lisa Kiely, Lauralea Kinser, and Mitra Motlagh.

Kendra Weddle Irons for writing the foreword and continued mentorship and encouragement since we met.

Athalya Brenner for assistance with Abravanel.

Gordon College professors Marvin R. Wilson and Lori Ambacher for igniting linked fascinations with Biblical scholarship and creative writing.

Paul R. Halupa for lighting the way to poetic imagination and all things literary.

The Mehl and Greene families for love and support.

Sam and Declan, my muses.

Introduction

Lady Midrash is inspired by the question, "what if?" If women were important to scripture's writers, or if the authors themselves *were* women, what would their stories reveal? How would received narratives change? Would we think about religion differently? As Rabbi Lynn Gottlieb asks in *She Who Dwells Within*, "How might women have told their stories if they were central, rather than peripheral, characters in the Bible?" Taking cues from Biblical oral tradition, as well as spoken word poetry and theatrical monologue, these poems explore the lives of Biblical women from their own points of view. Following in the footsteps of Jewish midrash, *Lady Midrash* re-examines the Bible's feminine voices, often marginalized by scripture's masculine dominant focus. Storytelling commentary via midrash allows the reader to interrogate scripture by what Michael Handelzalts describes as "filling in the many gaps left in the biblical narrative with respect to certain events and personalities that were only hinted at." Elisabeth Schüssler Fiorenza's "hermeneutic of liberative vision and creative imagination" empowers the creative artist to "actualize and dramatize biblical texts differently." Like Lady Wisdom in the book of Proverbs, *Lady Midrash* opens the doors to hidden truths and new understandings. The poems allow Biblical women to reclaim their own voices using a variety of methods.

Changing the Names

Many of the women's names have been modified from the most common transliterations and translations. This device of name variation serves to shake the reader out of ingrained traditional assumptions from the beginning of the poem. The new names help to remove familiarity that can block curiosity and obscure perspective.

In some cases, the traditional names of the women were Hebraicized by scripture, masking her cultural identity, and in a sense erasing her individuality. As the widow from Moab (present-day Jordan) becomes Ruth, she becomes a Jewish woman, losing the history of another place. Here

Introduction

she is renamed in Arabic, Raouda. In the poem, Raouda holds her grandson Jesse who will become the father of the king of Israel, and sings him Moabite lullabies. The Biblical story might assume she has forgotten her past, while the poem reclaims it. Similarly, Hagar becomes Hajar to reflect her Egyptian birth, and Zipporah becomes Saffūrah as Midian is located in modern-day Saudi Arabia. Women from what is now Palestine received a light Arabic modification of their names, for example Dabourah for Deborah, while the names of women from modern-day Israel often revert back to the Hebrew transliteration instead of utilizing the common English version, Ya'el for Jael, She'erah for Sherah, Khuldah for Huldah. Finally, since three matriarchs of the Abrahamic line are so exceptionally recognizable as Sarah, Rebecca, and Rachel, they might seem to have no new tales to tell. Here they are reimagined as Sahrai from Ur (modern Iraq), and Rebeqah and Rahela from Paddan-Aram (present-day Syria-Turkey border).

Names kept the same as in the English text were done so intentionally, often due to the expansive reputation of the woman in question and the contrasting interpretation taken by the poem. The Eve written of in *Lady Midrash* is markedly different from the well-known character in the Adam and Eve narrative. "Evil" queens Vashti (Esther) and Jezebel (Kings), and "prostitute" Rahab (Joshua) finally get a chance to speak from their own perspectives. Miriam becomes something of a scientist. Hannah is no longer a helpless woman accused of drunken behavior in the temple. Bathsheba is not the "adulterous" woman who seduces King David. Salome and Sapphira explain their actions. And Joseph receives a completely different reading from the typical interpretation.

Naming the Nameless

Many women in scripture are not named at all. Sometimes they are in the crowd, as in Matt 27:55, "There were also many women there, looking on from a distance, who had followed Jesus from Galilee, ministering to him" (ESV). At other times they are a singular focal point of the story and yet in some way out of focus. In this collection, some find their names in words. The lady commonly known as "Isaiah's wife" in Isaiah 8:3, is referred to in the original language using the word for female prophet, *nebiyah*. The text states she is the mother of Isaiah's children, but whether Isaiah and "Nebiyah" are married or not is a point of scholarly speculation, though the word prophetess is often less accurately translated simply as the prophet's wife. The Queen of Sheba in 1 Kings and 2 Chronicles is only referred to there by her title and country. Islamic tradition names her Bilqis. Taking a path between the traditions, her name here is Malikah, the Arabic word for queen, and a nod to the tradition that she might come from Yemen. The woman in Song of Songs or Song of Solomon receives the name Shulamith, inspired by her familiar title, "The Shulamite woman." In the Jephthah's Daughter poem, the speaker urges the reader to "Say her name for each year you remember," a purposely impossible task, since her name is not given by the text. She retains her unnamed status as a reminder of her victimization, written of but obscured in the telling. This collection serves to commemorate those who are often forgotten, saying the names of those we know, and even remembering lost names in absentia.

Overcoming Reputation

Among the most notorious women written in scripture are those who are misrepresented and unfairly demonized. Foreign women are often portrayed as sexually promiscuous (Rahab), evil (Jezebel), or simply in the wrong (Vashti). Jezebel's name becomes synonymous with great evil at the end times in Revelation. Even the Queen of Sheba, despite her state visit to Solomon's court receiving a brief mention in scripture, is the subject of the bedroom rumors in folklore, imagining a sexual relationship between her and the King of Israel. And Vashti's troubled reputation does not line up with her rather virtuous actions, as she opposes the royal demand to "display her beauty" before the king's drunken festivities. But women within the Abrahamic tradition also suffer from problematic reputations; perhaps the most infamous is Eve, written in Genesis as the singular cause of original sin. However, Eve's actions could be characterized as positively pursuing knowledge, taking an action that is commanded in Proverbs. From the New Testament, Mary Magdalene is traditionally branded a "prostitute," even though she was likely a leader in the early church and scripture never names any profession for her whatsoever. The women's stories in this collection that most resist their portrayals in scripture present the idea of authorial bias in the Bible.

Introduction

Recovering Cultural Identity

As mentioned above, women from outside modern-day Israel recover some of their cultural identity in changing their names from the Hebrew versions in the text. For Raouda, her Jordanian past forms the center of her poem. Saffūrah's poem remembers her relationship with God in her own landscape. For Hajar, it is important to remember her immigrant experience as one with considerable difficulties in a new country. All of these women who came from other places bear histories and secrets, gaps in their stories, as scripture shows us an incomplete portrait of them.

Shifting the Focus

Sometimes all that is necessary to see a story differently is to shift its focus. This method connects to Elisabeth Schüssler Fiorenza's "hermeneutic of remembrance" in *But She Said*. Is there someone else at the scene who does not speak? Is there someone else watching who does not appear to participate? What is not written down in this account? Whose perspective are we missing? Some women only receive a passing mention, but their stories are definitely worth repeating. Has there ever been a sermon on She'erah, the daughter of Ephraim who quietly built three cities? When we cross the Red Sea with Miriam instead of Moses, how is the journey different? If God speaks to Saffūrah rather than Moses, would the words sound the same? What if Isaiah's wife and not Isaiah had the vision of God's holiness? What if Chloe writes to rebuke Paul about his personal prejudices? Every poem in this collection uses the perspective shift to see women who are typically in the background or passed over.

Authorship

Another way women have been mistreated by the writers of scripture is the erasure of their accomplishments. If there were female authors of any parts of scripture, their attributions have not be preserved. However, looking at the Song of Songs, credited to Solomon with the title Song of Solomon, it seems reasonably possible that his lover the Shulamite woman (Shulamith) may have written it instead. As the book is almost entirely from her point of view, it seems rather likely that Solomon did not assume her voice for most of the poem, but rather that she wrote it herself. Fokkelien

Introduction

van Dijk-Hemmes suggests female origin or authorship of Ruth is possible, while Ruth Hoppin makes a case that the book of Hebrews in the New Testament might have been written by Priscilla. We may never achieve certainty on female authorship in scripture, but opening the question reveals the possibilities for silenced women's voices.

Genderswap

On stage, the tradition of characters played by opposite gender is as ancient as theater itself, but flipping the gender of familiar characters continues to cause vocal reactions from audiences. The cross-gender casting of male characters in television and film today is frequently met with purist uproar, from Starbuck in the *Battlestar Galactica* television reboot to Prospero in the film adaptation of *The Tempest* with Helen Mirren. Given the patriarchal environs of scriptural history, it would give no surprise if some of the "men" and "heroes" written of in the Bible were in fact women. This treatment has often been given to Junia of the New Testament as translators have often mistranslated her name as the masculine "Junias," finding the concept of a female apostle impossible. Experimenting with this theory, the poem on Joseph examines the evidence for a female "son" of Jacob, daughter of Rachel, following after Nurit Zarchi's short story, "And She Is Joseph."

Attributing Agency

Queen Vashti of the Esther story benefits from an imagined new ending in her poem as she takes control of her destiny, denying the king his "right," and denying him the full satisfaction of the punishment he might mete out in vengeance against his queen. Similarly instead of showing Rebecca as a pawn in the games of men, shipped to a new country at the behest of Abraham and Isaac, her choices and agency receive special care. In this case, a literary criticism style investigation of the text highlights her independent vivacious spirit, and little creative license or invention was necessary.

Conclusion

It is the hope of the author that these creative retellings encourage other creative minds in the hermeneutic of suspicion, proclamation, remembrance,

Introduction

and creative actualization. For those who acknowledge the aforementioned Biblical criticisms, a continued conversation with scripture will necessitate genuine wrestling with the text. We must dare to pit our imaginations against the gaps scripture leaves, especially where it concerns women which were clearly not of primary interest for scripture's writers, though for God there is neither Greek nor Jew, female nor male (Gal 3:28).

A Note about End Notes

It may seem unorthodox to open a book of poetry and discover a section of end notes in an otherwise creative work. However, it is the intention of the author for the notes to provide a unique portal into the references, resonances, and research that motivated the collection, in turn sending interested readers on Biblical, creative, and/or scholarly journeys of their own.

For general readers, the notes provide scripture references for Biblical passages used and cross-references to bring out similarities in story and juxtapositions in the text where relevant. For scholarly readers, the notes additionally show where poems engage with secondary literature and linguistic influences, largely from the Hebrew, Greek, and Arabic. Both sets of readers are encouraged to takes the poems both in their own context and also with the use of the supplementary information when embarking on a reading of this work.

Part I: **Tanakh**

Eve
(The first woman)

    Eve knew what she was doing.
    She saw the knowledge—
    life, breath,
    and understood the love,
5 that it was good.
    And there was evening
    and morning
    the seventh day.

    On her way out of the garden,
10 done picking fruit
    and naming things,
    she picked up a flaming sword
    of truth
    to crush a snake,
15 realizing she'd never kick the habit
    of discovery
    or names.

    Woman she was,
    she called the other, man,
20 since he was part of her
    but not all.
    She learned to cover herself
    against the world's thorns
    and saw to the care of its creatures,
25 its landscapes;

she walked with Wisdom,
she considered the universe
and love,
and saw that it was good.

Raouda
(Ruth)

Mo'ab, Mo'av . . .
Sleep, child, sleep.
I sing of lands
you will never know,
of swift sands that blow
across the dunes,
in a place I once called home.
Your father forgot
the words I taught him
far, so long ago
Your mother never saw the mountains
or Madaba's springtime flow
You are destined for
your grandfather's swiftness
And I see my smile
as you grow . . .
I teach you songs in a language
with sounds and echoes
I alone still know.

Vashti
(Queen of Persia)

The mystery uncovered,
the secret draping the hallways in whispers:
The king summons his queen.
The king calls for his possession.
5   Unveiled,
he commands
her beauty displayed.
Naked, to be gazed upon.
Like a star in the heavens.
10 Like a feast for the eyes.
It has always been so.

The command is immediate.
As is my disgust.
They say if I refrain,
15 other wives may rise up
and also disobey.
Is reigning power so fragile,
its spell broken by
the stasis of hennaed feet?
20 Can I speak a silent message
strong enough to reach
even half my people?

This is my duty,
beauty that subdues his stormy skies.
25 Show strength in acquiescence

I am advised,
But can honor withstand
a night's gaze?

My face is a flame,
my body a torch,
But I will not be scorched
by the fire,
and I will not be tamed.
I will not be used
to light this blaze.

The threat remains:
banished or tortured,
replaced by other wives.
Those who take lives might
extinguish the flame.

No.

Tomorrow
to save face,
I will be ordered
not to return.
That I will obey.
Let me vanish into starless night,
robed in modesty,
my name forever cloaked
in infamy.

Nebiyah
(The prophetess who bore Isaiah's children)

Hear *me*, you heavens!
Listen to *me*, earth!
For God has spoken,
spoken through me.
5   God spoke to Isaiah also,
but *I* birthed God's messages
in my body,
burning coal on my lips,
words in my mouth,
10 children in my arms.
Know this.

Therefore the Lord
will give you a sign:
a prophetess will conceive
15 and give birth
and will call the child Immanuel,
which means God With Us.
I did as I was told.

Take a great scroll
20 and write on it
with a woman's hand:
Go to the prophet,
conceive and bear
"the remnant," and "the plunder."
25 They will answer to these names

and in the echo
you will hear deafening wing claps.
Here am I, send me.

Another mother went to a prophet
30   and now her precious ones answer to
"without mercy"
and "not my people."
O Lord, how long?

And after all of this,
35   angels and infants,
visions and promises,
I was never his wife.

No eagles bore me up,
but I ran, ignoring weariness,
40   I walked and did not faint.
I carried the messages.
God was with me.
Perhaps one day
my strength will be renewed.

Hajar
(Hagar)

I am a cheap Egyptian vase,
once valuable,
with hieroglyphs you cannot read,
cracks you don't know are there,
You only notice me when you see
there is no water left
at the end of your journey.

I am the immigrant
who cleans your floors.
Queen of kicked-over buckets
and the washing
of whatever you have dirtied.
I am in your way,
under foot,
trodden,
and essential.

I hear your conversations.
I hear you denigrate my homeland.
The same place you departed wealthier
than before it bore your steps.
I hear you speak of me as of garbage.
I see the way you look at me, slant,
diminishing in your eyes, to dust.

"There is no water.

Come and fetch for us."
And my empty place will tell you:
run to the hills
when you find you are empty.
Find another stream.
Take to your feet.
Trust the stars.
Laugh, if you must.
Be brave.
But call me not.

My vase is fuller than I expected,
and also my eyes.
Like others who work for scraps,
my body was forfeit
the moment I lowered myself
to the ground,
the moment I cleaned your feet
the moment I fed you from my hand
the moment your eyes looked through me,
without a word.
Only a vase to carry your desires.

But God saw me in the desert,
A God I named,
A God who sees.
God saw me,
and God heard my child.
Even when you did not.

Ya'el
(Destroyer of Sisera)

The ibex slays the mountain
with a bowl of milk,
a gust of wind laps
at the tent flaps
5 to catch the last drops
from the mouth
of the fallen.
He will sleep deep,
affixed to the valley,
10 between her feet.
And a hundred trumpets
cannot wake him
The ibex alone
wields the hammer.

Jezebel
(Queen of Israel)

When the ground falls out beneath your feet . . .

        I put on my war paint

When they rename a god-fearing woman

        loose

        I tie my hair as I balance

                for today's audience

                      of one,

        risking death

        for grapes

            they say

When your feet burn near a makeshift altar . . .

        a magic trick

        of fire and smoke,

water and righteous anger,

15   make a city disappear in sea,

                    cover a queen in names,

                              let bronze dogs take

                                        her reputation

When the altar screams between the flames ...

20   shove your sword

      down its throat

          and cover the exit wound

                    with anointing oil,

                         or open your window

25   and scream

                                   back

When the flames sink in the morning sky ...

              drown the cedars

        and the lemon trees

30   until you've assassinated evil

with "truth"

and gravity

Jephthah's Daughter
(*The sacrifice*)

Every year we go out,
we climb the hills
wandering
as she did,
5   for four days,
she is celebrated
with night fires and songs,
with howling and hand-holding,
we stain our faces
10 with her favorite foods,
with the remnants
of laughing and memory.

We say her name.
We have not forgotten.

15 Say her name for each
year you remember.

Every year we go out,
we climb the hills
from whence her help
20 did not come,
for she was not Isaac,
nor was she Ishmael,
she was not delivered from the furnace,
without a ram in the brush,

without the voice of an angel,
without a burning hedge,
without the fourth in the fire,
documented
but without a name,
just a girl
a female sacrifice,
which in the temple
would mean nothing,
less than nothing.

Slain without an altar,
we remember this daughter
we remember her face
we remember her voice.

Say her name for each
year you remember.

Rahab
(*A woman of Jericho*)

I could kill Joshua.
And his spies.
Yes I chose sides.
What of it?
My city fell.
Who wants to fall with it?
They kept their bargain,
my family walked free.
But the account
they made—
I wouldn't know?
Please.
I wouldn't find out?
as they told and retold
the taking of the fragrant city,
together with their men
laughing over spoils of war
the "giants" they saw
the plunder they took
the women they plundered
there was this one—
a harlot with a golden heart,
she helped us,
hid us in her rooms
in the day
and at night—
she was so fine,

flax bales and linen
all over her apartment
30 jewelry
and gold
no typical lady
-in-waiting.
War is heaven,
35 you know?

Never mind the looms
the lady wove at all day,
and many times all night
spinning linen thread
40 in the moon city,
while it stood.
You think flax is cheap?

Never mention the family
also in her rooms,
45 the children we shushed
when the city guards came,
or the chaff straw animals
made by spies for crying eyes,
these were not showcased
50 mementos of epic espionage,
though the small things
and quiet,
may well have saved their lives.

And about that red cord?
55 Dyed fabric I wove,
the same kind that bought
my family's bread,

cloth stewing in roots and insects
the unholy color
60 of ordinary blood
I sent this cloth out my window
And I should have known.
Surely I ignited
their red-fabric district
65 fabrication
with my welcome hand

She signaled to us—
to come up—
to her room!—
70 Boys.

She'erah
(The builder)

Footnote
or parenthetical:
a daughter of Ephraim,
hardly worth mentioning
with *sons* on every hill,
SHOUTING for attention,

    She'erah

    BUILT

    Upper

    and Lower

    Beth Horon

    AND

    Uzzen-She'erah

Just three cities,
the last of which
she named:

HEAR SHE'ERAH.

Shulamith
(*The beloved of Solomon*)

Who is this
rising like the dawn
aurora,
bright as the moon shining
5   clear as pure sunlight,
daunting

Winds and zephyrs
awake!
I belong to the song
10   and the song is mine:
From me,
to my beloved.

Arise and come—
gazelle-leap over mountains,
15   through spring rains,
across vineyards,
sail through the sea of roses,
to meet me,
once again.

Miriam
(The prophetess)

With experience
taking *out* of the water,
and assuring safe passage *through*,
Miriam sang with tambourine,
5 before she introduced
red algae *into* the Nile.

Her brothers could argue over
who stood on the shore
with arms outstretched,
10 but meanwhile Miriam
felt the gale force winds
begin to sweep the sea
and the reeds.

As they crossed,
15 Miriam led,
following the Shekinah.
Had God spoken only
through Moses?

Saffūrah
(Zipporah)

    Now in Arabia
    Saffūrah was keeping the flock
    and led them
    past the snakes,
5 past the rocks,
    to the wilderness of God
    flown high with birds,
    to the crown of the ridge.
    And there was a volcanic vent
10 near an acacia tree
    which burned
    but was not consumed,
    out of this God called to her,
    Saffūrah, Saffūrah!
15 And she said,
    Here I am.
    And God said,
    Stand here
    with your bare feet,
20 which are holy
    because I made them.
    I AM the God of your mother,
    The God of Hajar,
    The God of Sahrai,
25 The God of Rebeqah,
    The God of Bilhah, Zilpah,
    Rahela and Leah.

And Saffūrah did not hide
her face from God.

30 Then God said,
I have surely seen
the affliction of my people everywhere,
and have heard their hissing cries,
and their hard howls.
35 I know their sufferings.
Those in Egypt,
those in Israel,
those in Yemen,
those in Iraq,
40 those in Syria,
those in Palestine.

Khuldah
(*Huldah*)

All the curses are written in this book,
on these gates
near the mount,
on these walls
5   without tunnels:
destruction,
chaos,
prophesied.

Thus says El,
10 I will bring disaster upon this place
and its inhabitants.
They turned their faces away
from an omnipresent God.
They made offerings
15 to gods that are not God.

Thus says El,
they provoke anger
with the work of their hands
which I foresaw.

20 Thus says El,
they provoke my wrath,
unquenchable.
But because you have a tender heart
and because you are humble

25 and because you weep oceans
   because I hear you
   you will die in peace.
   Your eyes will be saved
   from the disaster
30 I bring upon your children
   and your children's children.
   This is the word of the Lord.
   Thanks be to God.

Dabourah
(Deborah)

Lady fire,
woman of torches
and words like hornets,
holding court,
5 judging a nation
at a palm tree
named after
herself

   At her command
10 thousands of men
go fight the enemy
as she accompanies
her general
for his assurance.
15 Even at the battle
she commands him,
her plans
collaborate
with the ibex

20 Woman of flames
and words like wasps,
they sing the victory
named after
herself

Hannah
(The mother of Samuel)

In the still light of Shiloh,
this is between You and I,
no brush of cloth,
just breath,
no witnesses,
just longing and wrung eyes,
no sound from my lips,
just yearning
from the temple,
so that striving to be heard,
from earth to heaven,
no one can take this prayer
from me,
from us.

A drunk old man
stumbles between,
put your wine away,
I could say to him,
how long will *you* be
intoxicated?

But no, I am praying.
Was praying.
Am praying.
Life is prayer.
All things are praying.

I look up and dissent,
as You taught me.
I am not who he thinks.
I am a woman
who honors
her commitments.

I reserve my strength
as he imagines the right
to deny or grant wishes,
djinn disguised as priest.

I know You and I have dealt,
before the interruption:
a difficult bargain,
to receive,
only to give back.
But You keep your promises
and listen.
As do I.

Malikah
(*Queen of Sheba*)

Their eyes meet,

        one wisdom to another,

    a thousand impossibilities

        thrumming

          dangling

            simmering

      from every corner

           of the throne room.

    Queen of the South,

        Yemeni,

          Ethiopian,

            Or Djinni.

She poses questions

      and circles answers,

15 watching as he watches

        the tigers,

                her honor guard,

            with questions of their own.

Her last riddle

20   he cannot solve

          and she disappears.

            On camels?

                Or on a carpet?

                      Or both?

25   A final paradox.

    Queen of the South,

        Yemeni,

           Ethiopian,

                Or Djinni.

Bathsheba
(The mother of Solomon)

My sons.
My heart.
You are all that remains
in this life of ashes.

5 Shobab, I have been a captive
Shamua, but God heard me
Nathan, you were a gift
Solomon, I was made whole

I can give you
10 nothing
but histories of violence
blotted out,
and proverbs
erased
15 from a former life
wiped clean
off the map,
ripped from the scroll
shattered

20 But remember this
while you live,
if only traces
and fragments remain,
if ever you are summoned

25 to burn a chapter
and start anew,
now writing
in charcoal,
now building
30 on ruins:

hear instruction,
seek wisdom,
act with valor
and kindness
35 in all things,
and if you are fortunate,
perhaps you will be honored
with an *eshet chayil* love
besides mine.

40 May you be blessed
forever,
beloved sons of rape.

Sahrai
(Sarah)

Why did Sahrai laugh?
Why did you not
tell her of the promise?
Did you not believe Me?
5 Did you think it would not
come to pass?
Do you think I promise lightly
and the message was not
worthy of sharing
10 with the Mother of the covenant?
You fell on your face laughing before,
but surely you believe now.

And Abraham was silent.

Why did Sahrai laugh?
15 She knows nothing is impossible
for Me
who gave birth
to the universe.

And Sahrai answered.

20 Beyond hope
beyond despair
I had given away
any thought

of fulfillment
25 long ago.
When I heard the word
the laughter was rising
within me
bubbling beneath the surface
30 of a newly sprung stream
in a world of sand

I laughed in awe.

Ah, but you did laugh.

Rebeqah
(Rebecca)

She goes where she will.

Rebeqah follows the foreigner with his camels
to the well.
It doesn't take a genius
5   to know what he wanted
when he mutters
to himself
I will be released from this oath
if no woman is willing to go
10 I will be released from this oath
if a woman waters these camels
I will be released!

She would run back and forth
to give him
15 all the drink he wanted
and water those camels
as many jars as it took—
anything to get out of Paddan-Aram.

It was easy to convince
20 her brother Laban to let her go
for a little of the gold.
She wouldn't need any
if she just got her own
ship of the desert.

25　She goes to the well
　　and draws the future:
　　sunset in a new land,
　　a meditating man in a field,
　　silken tents—
30　twins—
　　speaking to God
　　and God speaking back.

Rebeqah follows the foreigner with his camels.

She goes where she will.

Rahela
(Rachel)

Because there is no honor
among thieves,
because you think
you can't con a con
5   because my henchwoman grievances
fall below your notice
because I cannot rise
to your devious level
because the way of women
10 is upon me now
and the day I was born
because this is my inheritance
from you—
justice by other means,
15 knocking over the house,
and because my sister Leah dared me,
(yet another trickster):

they are all gone away.

I sit upon your precious idols,
20 defile them with blood
or sanctify them
with deceit,
slipping them under your nose
with the easiest play
25 a woman ever made—

taboo trumps all,
and Jacob's curse
may find its mark yet
even when I am searched
30 and no one
finds the stolen goods
with me.

Raised by treachery,
wed to trickery,
35 betting a life for a life,
it is no surprise
when I lose
in the only game
I desperately need to win.
40 A fool's barter—
The house takes it all.

Joseph
(The first child of Jacob and Rachel)

What if
she *is* Joseph?

When the favorite wife,
previously barren,
5   finally gives birth
to her one and only
at the time,
why does she
ambiguously name
10 her first child
"an addition"
rather than "son of my sorrows"
or "son of my right hand"
or "at last a son!"
15 or son and anything?
The all-important son!
Male child
sent from heaven!
She is saved!
20 God has heard her prayer!
A son in the balance
against her sister.

Is the only way
to have the child she wants
25 a lie about the child she has?

Born of a "beautiful" mother,
"Beautiful" Joseph:
in the long sleeved garment
of Tamar and kings' daughters,
30 conveniently clean-shaven in Egypt,
jailed but alive after Potiphar's wife,
with no name of a tribe
which passes instead through sons,
accepting "the blessing of the breasts
35 and of the womb"
from *his* father?
"Joseph is a fruitful vine."
And the grandsons are born
upon Joseph's knees
40 like the children of Bilhah
on his mother's knees.

Zaphnath-paaneah,
revealer of dreams,
secret revealer,
45 dreamer of secrets,
and secret keeper.

Shekinah
(God)

The Spirit of El,
She made me.
And the breath of
El Shaddai
5   the strong
does not destroy,
ehyeh asher ehyeh
She keeps me alive.

Who can speak
10 for the Shekinah?

A mother in labor
A mother who gives birth
A mother who nurses
A mother who comforts her child
15 as God does.

Who can speak
for the Shekinah?

Who is like the Lord?
A woman who helps a child walk
20 An eagle spreading her wings over young
A woman who searches for something lost
as God does.

The Spirit of El,
She made me.
25 And the breath of
El Shaddai
the strong
does not destroy,
ehyeh asher ehyeh
30 She keeps me alive.

Noadiah

(The prophetess)

(graffiti on a half-built wall)

HEY! NEHEMIAH!

YOU WANT TO GO?

I'M READY

5 MEET @ THE WALL

YOU'LL ANSWER TO ME

AND YHWH

REGARDS,

Irit
(*The wife of Lot*)

A rear guard does not gaze;
she keeps watch,
as sulfur rains,
following a fearful frontman
5   she takes care not to lose anyone
she can protect,
don't go back for her.

What might seem to be
a look at the forbidden
10 through a saline veil,
like the desirous bite
of disintegrating fruit,
is so much more distant than that taste,
to see the past clearly,
15 from the mountain
without bonds,
in order to move on.

Screams pursue her,
and not him, who is
20 unencumbered by their memory
of last night,
slamming doors
reaching for anyone
to throw to a mob,
25 anyone to leave behind.

They pass a pillar,
a warning,
THIS is what will happen to you
if you turn back
30 if you even falter
you will be abandoned,
deliverance annulled.

They walk on,
and she carries the threats
35 she's been handed,
sweating salt
climbing fast
keeping up with angel pace
and they reach the promised place.

40 A man explains his wife's absence
as a cruel miracle,
in his drunkenness
he might believe the lie,
accidentally testifying
45 to her worth in cost,
a priceless loss.

Remember,
whoever tries to restrain her
will lose her.

50 Two will be in one bed,
one will take her things and go,
the other will be left.

Remember,
no one tells Abraham
not to look.

Yidana
(The witch of Endor)

    Some call me a witch,
    which would be illegal
    if it were true,
    which is impossible
5 because witches
    aren't real
    so therefore it is untrue
    this unreal thought
    that I am a witch.

10 I do get paid
    on occasion
    to tell the truth
    of what I know
    which helps my reputation
15 as a witch
    because women being prophets
    is mostly illegal
    it being impossible
    for women
20 to tell the truth
    and pull no switches
    or punches and not be labeled
    —witches.

    Sometimes I help kings
25 find dead men

Sometimes I tell kings
they *are* dead men
or dead men they are kings
of course it wasn't me,
30   a witchy woman
what do I know of these things?
I assume the guise of another prophet
even if he is deceased
and suddenly my words gain gravitas
35   using a subtle cheat
We can circumvent your laws
and break them together,
which is funny
since you banished
40   women who tell you things
yet search us out
when you notice Azrael's wings

I'll see dead people,
be dead people
45   I'll tell you what you need to hear,
Maybe I'm just here to spite you,
and curse you, which
you never know nor
care in the end, or
50   maybe I'm simply the *prophet*
you send for
rather than "witch"
in the village of Endor

Tamar
(The three)

Ta·mar′:

Tamarind
Tamarisk
Tamarah

5 Three date palms
in a scandalous line,
swaying, rocking, dancing,
in time
monuments to movement,
10 changing course,
and bending without breaking,
the song through their leaves
plays in the storm

Tamarind
15 Tamarisk
Tamarah

Piquant Tamar,
the salacious,
the provocative,
20 the righteous,
married sons of Judah
until she got sons
of her own

in her own way,
rising up, and
breaking through.

Rugged Tamar,
the salt cedar,
the steadfast,
the survivor,
persisted in standing up
to the tempest,
to the faithless,
she is wise in the thunder,
eloquent in the deluge.

Last Tamar,
least of these,
a small tree in the shadow
of two,
looking up at the sky,
imagining Hazezon,
and Mazandaran and Yazd
not yet built
but for their fortresses
planned in clouds,
she whispers the memory
of every Tamar she knows

Tamarind
Tamarisk
Tamarah

Delilah
(The beloved of Samson)

Thread my hair
through bowstrings
and uprooted gates,
hanging low
5   amidst the silvery vines
of your tangled heart,
tossed into a thunderous river
in the middle of the night,
as foxes light fires
10 on either side
with razors looming overhead,
and we unravel the knot
of our twisted bed.

Riddled with holes
15 from which your secrets flow,
wholly a riddle with such strength
and weakness intertwined.
One question you never ask
your little doll,
20 your dahlia,

Why?

What terrible place was I in
that I lay down on the altar
with you for a fee

25 so easily?

> Never were you so blind
> as the day you first
> caught sight of me.

Peninnah
(*Wife of Elkanah*)

Do I exist?

Straw-woman and all
my invented straw-children
sidle up to the temple
5   to receive invented portions
as I cackle in delight,
some harpy first wife
without soul
pure bite,
10 a cornerstone
of any birth fable,
my fertility abilities
supersede acceptability
for our heroine, (notably,
15 the author's mother).

Am I a disposable woman
done away with
in the slash of a pen?
inciting despair
20 with my ample wordlessness
and my womb,
a champion after the example
of Leah and others?
Who remembers my rosy hair
25 or any of my children's names,

how I lacerated idiot priests
with a single brittle glare?
No such fame or shame.

Since my actions take place offstage,
and this monologue may be fake,

I wait between the pages,

and betwixt each

line's

break.

Women of the Decalogue
(Women at Sinai)

And Moses said to *all* the people:
Be ready for the third day,
everyone,
go not near a woman.

5 An impossible feat
more than the most perilous climb,
to go not near oneself,
if you are a woman,
hearing these words,
10 waiting to approach God,
asking: unsex me here,
to unmake
what God has made
and called good.

15 When we go with Moses
we must be other than ourselves,
somehow,
incompatible as we are
with God's theophany
20 these days
ill-equipped to be what we ought
or should.

But before Moses
God had no difficulties with us,

25 speaking directly
to Hajar
and Sahrai
and Rebeqah
to name a few
30 along the way.

Are we suddenly so unclean,
so tainted by our gender
at all times
it is impossible for God
35 to commune with us
just now?
Or is the covenant
not meant for us at all?

But when God spoke with these women
40 named here
about the issue of their wombs,
and drew near to them,
where they were,
in raw places
45 not at all serene,
this is clearly not a God afraid
of becoming unclean.

Serakh bat Asher
(Daughter of Jacob's son Asher)

I rub her hands with oil and myrrh
while she prays for the world.
No one knows how old she is for sure:
she isn't my mother's
5   great grandmother,
or hers.

I hold her hands
and her green eyes are alight,
the woman of crossed bones
10 and skulls,
fearless, ruthless
wise woman of Abel
daughter of Asher bin Zilpah,
historian of our people.

15 Her hands are gnarled
but their strength endures
carrying names and stories
all this time,
through all these lands,
20 and each year new babies are born
continuing the line,
and her repertoire expands.

She never asks when
my husband and I

25 might finally conceive
and not because most have given up,
she just smiles and asks
to take the pain, my hands in hers
pakod pakadti—
30 God remembers you.

She is Methuselah, Enoch,
Noah, and Elijah,
there is no compare to her
among women

35 I hope one day she holds
my daughter or son
and gives her blessing
as she has done
for others
40 but who knows
maybe God or Eden
or a fiery chariot will sweep
her up without death
since it has not come for her yet.

Part II: **New Testament**

Kalima
(The Syro-Phoenician woman)

Did you hear that?
Did He just say
what I thought He said?
You all heard Him!
Is the Son of God
this fully human?
How socially-constructed
is your Savior?
Does he see race?
Or gender?
Does he speak
Slurs?
Epithets?
Does he find
dogs under the table?
Salukis begging for scraps
or feral animals
fighting in the gutter,
dirty beasts in the street
who belong nowhere?

To be human
is to have these thoughts,
To be divine
is to learn from them?
(a process theologian?)

He did listen.
Eventually.

My daughter was healed.
Eventually.

But I still can't believe
like so many others before
He called me a bitch.

Shahar
(The woman accused of adultery)

At dawn I appear
like in a duel
between the olive trees
in the courtyard
5 dragged in by accusers
who were there,
not so much bystanders
but participants
I can barely stand
10 after what they've done to me
and now they reach
for boulders
to bury me
with their sins.

15 The rabbi leans down
to write on the ground
each of their names,
the ones who did this,
He doesn't use my name,
20 keeping this distance
in dialogue
but reminds me to look up
to the sun rising:
no one else is left.

25 Go now and leave

their sins
behind you.

Maryam an-Nasiri
(Mary, mother of Jesus)

A dangerous affair
getting pregnant
even if you were married
which I wasn't
5 so I had to run away
so far from my home
it would take days
unchaperoned
as I was
10 kicked out,
too bad the angel of God
couldn't stay for the pregnancy
like many would-be
not-fathers
15 of my time
and yours
only bothering
about conception
and those sorts
20 of details,
good thing I had a cousin
who wouldn't judge,
her husband might have spoken up
and brought all Hebron
25 down on my head,
but he couldn't speak
at least that was convenient,

unlike the birth outside the inn
or waiting to be purified
30 days after bearing
the perfect,
Holy
son of God

Anna
(*The prophetess*)

Behold:

A righteous women's words
are full of grace
discarded, disregarded,
5 as promised,
devout turtledoves
that flew away,
pigeons that escaped,
uneaten loaves of bread,
10 just the pieces remain.

Behold:

A righteous man's words
are remembered,
written down,
15 a light for revelation,
a marvelous blessing,

But this is half of a pair
for her pair of eyes
has seen salvation
20 also.

Old women's stories,
they call wives' tales

old men's stories
they call history
and I suppose in this case—
it is his side
of the tale
which remains,
which continues

refuse, and abstain
from the profane,
from the insipid
fables of women

others might recognize these,
if they had the chance,
as wisdom

Salome
(*The dancer*)

I see him die
without peace
like his cousin
alone though we were there
5 *Eloi, Eloi, lema sabachthani?*
I see him forsake us
in that moment
but I wonder
why I was forsaken
10 in my youth
alone though others were there
dancing my last dance
on the blade of a knife
for a lecherous king
15 and stepfather
an honor to no one
pawn in a game
between dark king
and the red queen
20 as they cried
off with his head
I could not say his name
but I see him die
without peace
25 like his cousin
alone though we were there
Eloi, Eloi, lema sabachthani?

　　　　as I dance
　　　　the lyrics to the song
30　　repeat

　　　　And as I appear at the tomb
　　　　I wonder
　　　　whose death
　　　　I must suffer next
35　　*Eloi, Eloi, lema sabachthani?*

Junia
(The apostle)

My name is threatening
so you change it?
J U N I A + S
Isn't there a curse on those
5 adding to the scroll?
A single letter builds a man:
who knew creation was so simple?

And if you don't change my name
you remove apostleship
10 J U N I A − vocation
Isn't there a curse on those
subtracting from the scroll?
The deduction demotes a woman,
and her denigration *is* that simple,
15 even for one who came before
the most renowned apostle.

Samara

(The Samaritan woman)

At high noon
at the well
another duel:

Go call your husband
5 He says,
knowing

Go marry his brother
They say,
knowing

10 Go marry his brother
They say,
knowing

Go marry his brother
They say,
15 knowing

Go marry his brother
They say,
knowing

it is the law
20 to be owned thusly,
and if you break the cycle

and call not your husband
or his brother
who has charge over you
25   if you worship in a place
they tell you is unsacred
if you are thirsty
dying for water
at noon
30   you are willing to go
in the heat
of the sun

the least He could do
is not tell me to go,
35   knowing

Philip's Daughters
(Four women who prophesied)

    In the coffee shops
    of Caesarea
    and on the coast
    at the marina
5 at the sea,
    at the harbor
    at the theater,
    at the theological library
    four daughters
10 proclaim God's message
    for the future
    four daughters prophesy
    four daughters of wonders
    four daughters
15 lift up their voices
    in the coffee shops
    of Caesarea
    and on the coast
    at the marina

Nuntia
(The wife of Pilate)

In my dreams
I had blood in my palms
In my dreams
I was falling through an ocean
of vinegar
In my dreams
it was my side torn apart
and my feet were ripped
from the center
In my dreams
I bore the terrors
of the world
every ill thought
each hateful deed
was crushed into my head
the heaviest weight
I struggled to carry
though the streets
as I was spat upon
by heaven and earth
and under the earth.

When I awoke
no one believed
anything I said,
prophesy
or no

It was just a nightmare
go back to sleep

As if it were possible
to ever sleep sound
to ever close my eyes
in peace
again

The Maji
(Wise travelers from the East)

    We had all seen the star,
    as foretold
    by the prophetess,
    where we were
5 which might be East
    of where this is read
    perhaps
    but it also could be North
    or South
10 or West

    We three set out
    it is true

    BISHAKHA, from India:
    My gift was myrrh
15 which is the scent
    of the stars
    if they were given one,
    my blessing is bitter
    knowing what is to come

20 MALEKJAHAN, from Persia:
    I took a gold censor,
    a fitting token from
    a self-proclaimed
    queen of the world,

25　my blessing glitters
　　but is heavy
　　knowing what is to come

　　GHAZIYAH, from Arabia:
　　I brought frankincense
30　from my country
　　to burn
　　a sweet aroma
　　which must die
　　to live

35　All these things spoke to the future,
　　royal gifts
　　and burial perfumes
　　After all, we are wise women
　　and God spoke to us in our dreams

40　We returned another way
　　and wished you well
　　as you were about to flee
　　with your mother
　　to Egypt
45　and would need to sell something
　　valuable
　　for passage
　　to get you there

　　We understood this
50　and went East

Niyyah
(The woman with the alabaster jar)

    While Jesus was at
    the village of poverty,
    Bayt Anya
    in the West Bank
5 he was not the only prophet
    in the room,
    someone else understood
    the ministry,
    the purpose,
10 the destiny,
    all the signs
    pointing toward the cross-
    roads coming,
    someone else knew
15 what was coming
    for them all,
    someone else
    whose deeds were remembered
    to some degree
20 just an ember,
    but no one promised
    her name would be remembered
    perhaps lost in the rush
    of the trial
25 historical memory is strange,
    porous as alabaster
    pungent as nard

what a waste
to spill out
30 the beautiful wisdom
of a prophet
who reads life and death
in an undersized vial

Sapphira
(*The woman accused of fraud*)

Blue sapphire
of a crystal tear
marbled
lapis lazuli
5   as you were caught
between heaven
and earth,
master of church
and earthly master
10 deceit in the tithe
in the marriage
complicit perhaps
or co-opted
who will know—
15 as God shot first

and we ask
questions afterward

Joanna
(Wife of Herod's chief of staff)

Because they have not happened
to you,
our stories sound like nonsense
not experiences, but
5 idle tales
unreliable
ridiculous fantasy
unworthy,
without truth.

10 If you want to be radical
followers in the tradition
of Christ
(who we saw alive again
before you did)
15 believe women
when they tell you
what their life's been through,
what they've been witness to:
we're not delirious,
20 what we describe
might be outside
your experience.

Shoshan
(Susanna)

Was my gospel lost
in the fire
at Alexandria?
A burned lotus,
5 destroyed lily
in the library
rose no more,
listed
and that is all,
10 Shoshan:
the only history
of my holdings
is a lone scrap
in the charred
15 card catalogue drawer:
WITHDRAWN

Damaris
(An Athenian)

You can attempt
to break a rocky hill
like Areopagos,
and have a go
5   at making the place straight, level,
and narrow
for a gentler person,
bring the high place low,
iron out mistakes,
10 rough edges,
stumbling blocks,
anything that might get in your way,
furrow your brow,
or sow discord.

15 You can try to tame the gods of war,
dull her spears, satisfy his hunger,
if you can,
imagine you will not be overwhelmed
simply by the invocation.

20 You can subdue a name
with a minor alteration
exchanging subduer for subdued
in ink
and blur the named into the unknown

25 Take a stab.

    But the rocks haven't moved,
    not one great stone
    from the hillside,
    this is Hellas.

30 Drink to my health
    if you like
    toast me like a mantra
    but if you say nothing else
    about what I did or said
35 or who I am,
    or where I'm from,
    for Athena's sake,
    call me Damasandra

Rhoda
(*A slave*)

They said
you are out of your mind!
What does a slave know?
But who has the last laugh now?
5   The thorns?
Or she
who was out of her mind,
the rose?

If you don't believe me,
10 the man can wait
at the gate.

Tabitha
(A disciple)

A woman scholar
Mathētria from Jaffa
Disciple

Dead

5 in the service of the good
in the service of the poor

As adoring women wave the tapestries
and wave the weaving
she wove,

10 Tabitha, gazelle, get up
and weave some more

Laishah & Eunike
(The grandmother and mother of Timothy)

Women who were not silent in the church,
or at home,
everywhere
raising up
5 training up
others in the Way,
we knew
there were many.
If they had kept silent
10 the rocks would cry out
urging them to teach.

Their victory will be announced
with the roar of the lioness,
proclaiming the names
15 of their children
and their grandchildren
after their own.

Mariam al-Majdal
(Mary Magdalene)

Mariam of Qaryat al-Majdal
Apostle to the Apostles
a girl from al-Jalīl
before it was ethnically cleansed,
the girl with seven demons
worth of chronic illness
not a sexual "sin"
not a sex worker
not an adulteress
or even if she was
just someone in need of healing,
healed enough to receive
the first visitation
of the God
who rose
from death
like the girl
with both feet in the grave
now well
from Qaryat al-Majdal

Prisca
(*Priscilla*)

God alone knows.
The Ancient of Days
wrote what happened
in Her book of Life.

5 I own
a conspicuous name
withstanding time
in a conspicuous order:
Top billing, if you will.

10 Yet here we also have
a conspicuous absence:
God knows,
other names would not be lost
or lent out
15 so carelessly.

Phoebe
(A deacon)

Radiant,
Pure,
Bright,
Action hero,
5 Deacon.

Phoebe:
courier of the letter
commended to you now
as she found her way into the city
10 with a dangerous document
prophet
messenger
prostatis
she has been my teacher
15 and instructed many others

Radiant,
Pure,
Bright,
Action Hero,
20 Phoebe.

Ilisabaʻ
(Elizabeth)

In the days of Maltháki,
queen of Yahuda
there was a priestess named Ilisabaʻ
in al-Khalīl
5   a daughter of Harun.
She had a husband
and they were righteous
walking blameless
but they had no child,
10 not because they were advanced in years
but rather it was feared
her man, as it happened
was barren.

Now while she was serving as priestess
15 before God
she was chosen to enter the temple
and burn incense
and the angel of God
appeared to Ilisabaʻ:

20   I know this
        as I stand in the presence of God,
        your prayer has been heard—
        your husband
        will give you a child
25   at last,

she said,

> not that you were incomplete before
> but God will honor the desires of your heart
> which She considers
> pure

Candace
(Queen of Ethiopia)

Hanging out in Gaza,
the queen of Meroë
goes up the road
in her chariot
5   having left her plazas
in disguise.
She claims to be
her own treasurer.
People assume eunuch
10 when she's dressed like this
which has worked to explain
a few things
more easily
in the past,
15 in the abyss
of truth and lies
and what the observers miss,
she doesn't correct
what they surmise.

20 The kandake
asks for answers
from the man of God,
as she reads Isaiah
in the original language,

25 her seventh.

"Do you understand?"
he assumes she does
not
he assumes she is not wise
30 to the text

She feigns misunderstanding
in her sixth language
"How can I understand
unless someone
35 explains it to me?"
a hint of sarcasm

but the Angel of the Lord
urges her to keep talking
to this man
40 who misunderstands
and keep his
conversation
while she knows
what the passage is

45 as you teach a child
by asking questions,
asking to be taught
in turn

he wants to baptize her
50 She gives orders to stop
the chariot
unrehearsed
but when they come up

out of the water
55 the Spirit takes the man
away
just before he can see
who he has immersed

Rejoicing for the good news of
60 vital mission accomplished,
the warrior queen heads home
adding "preacher of Meroë"
to her many titles

Bracha

(The woman who blessed the mother of Jesus)

Caught up in the miracle:
demons expelled
and victory for good,
a woman finds her voice
5   in blessing,

honoring the Savior
and the one who carried
and raised Him
to be who He is
10 on earth.

But His reply expels her blessing
with a word
and future doom
dismantling her in pieces:
15 a time will come to favor
wombs that never bore
and breasts that never nursed.

May those who bless you
be blessed.

The "Other" Mary
(One of many)

A few of us had the same name
spoken in the air
sung from afar
Mary
Mara
Mariam
Miriam
Maryam
Marium
Meriam

Bitterness in Hebrew
mar
or
Love in Egyptian
mer
which truth
do you choose?
or is there bittersweet
truth
in both?

It may get confusing
for the Marks and Johns
and John Marks:

A multitude of women,

25 an entire bazaar
barred from writing
their own stories
marred also
by a shared moniker,
30 identity married
to their toponym or patronym,
some way to distinguish
to understand
to break monotony
35 of Marthas, Marys, Miriams
all of us pursing our lips
in a bilabial consonant
almost-smile
about to speak
40 our own name,
to spar with m and r
with *mu* (μ) or *mem* (מ) or *mīm* (م)
and the small scar
of *resh* (ר) or *raa* (ر)
45 perhaps with *theta* (θ) or
the three dots of *thaa* (ث),

Which in no way
tells
precisely
50 who
we
are

Kyria
(Beloved lady of Second John)

Lady, loved of God,
in Efes
esteemed *hanımefendi*,
have mercy,
5   I am
only writing to you now
the elect
mistress of the church
in Selçuk
10 and all of İzmir
I hope you have not lost anything
in the waiting,
and have not been waiting long

I would rather we speak in person
15 so I may receive the reward
of your wisdom,
our joy may be complete,
and truth may abide with us
I would rejoice to see you again
20 Grace, mercy and peace be with us both
in truth and love
in different places

your chosen sister
sends her blessings
25 and I do
as well

Martha
(Sister of Mary and Lazarus)

Diákonos:
Runner.
She who kicks up dust
She who pursues
5 She who hastens after
She who carries out
She who moves
She who ministers

    She ALSO
10 learns at the feet of the master
and like all ministers
she serves also,
but the *diákonos*
asks questions
15 stirs up trouble
stirs up the earth
speaks for herself
asserts her influence
calls out her sisters
20 and brothers—

If we move this discussion
to where the serving takes place
we can work *and* listen
with one another.

Tryphaena & Tryphosa
(God's workers)

    Salute Tryphaena
    Salute Tryphosa
    Salute the delicate
    the luxurious
5   the dangerously swift
    greet the nymph
    welcome Eden
    nod to the queen of Thrace
    and her sister,
10 women discipled not by Paul
    but by Thecla

Lysia
(A sister of Jesus)

Is this not Joseph's daughter?
Verily I say unto you
no prophet is accepted
in her own country

5 or any country

his sisters didn't need to look for him
we were already there
Maria
Lydia
10 Anna
Salome
and Lysia
listening to our brother
the prophet
15 the other brothers
could not accept
the one all the other sheaves
would bow down to
the one who had dreams
20 the one who was not like the others,
we knew better
and we do the will of God in heaven
and we are his sisters
written out of the story

Chloe
(A leader of the church in Corinth)

From Chloe,
called by God's will to be an apostle
of Jesus Christ

To Paulos,
5   our brother:
Grace and peace to you.

We beg you
in the name of our Savior,
to agree in your message,

10 And do not support factions,
divisions, and disunities
between sisters and brothers.

You have been saying
A woman's head must be covered
15 when she prophesies

and yet you say in the same letter
women must be silent
in the church

You have many words
20 about how women may clothe their bodies
and link this with submission and authority

But to the church in Ankara
you write: there is neither male nor female.
No longer Jew nor Greek
25 (perhaps important since they are neither).

If we are one in Christ—
(you are right
that we are)
should I instruct you on your garments?
30 should I tell you when you may speak?

Should I advise you in your choices,
"I would hope that everyone (you Paulos)
could be like me (Chloe)"?

Be fully engaged in the work of Jesus,
35 be on your guard about your personal prejudices,
and steadfastly pursue equality.

Amen.

Abbreviations

Bible Translations

ESV	English Standard Version
JPS	Jewish Publication Society 1917
KJV	King James Version
NASB	New American Standard Bible
NIV	New International Version
NKJV	New King James Version

Book Abbreviations

Acts	Acts
1–2 Chr	1–2 Chronicles
1–2 Cor	1–2 Corinthians
Dan	Daniel
Deut	Deuteronomy
Esth	Esther
Exod	Exodus
Ezek	Ezekiel
Gal	Galatians
Gen	Genesis
Hab	Habakkuk
Heb	Hebrews
Hos	Hosea
Isa	Isaiah

Abbreviations

Jer	Jeremiah
Job	Job
John	John
1–2–3 John	1–2–3 John
Josh	Joshua
Judg	Judges
1–2 Kgs	1–2 Kings
Lev	Leviticus
Luke	Luke
Mark	Mark
Matt	Matthew
Mic	Micah
Neh	Nehemiah
Num	Numbers
Prov	Proverbs
Ps	Psalms
Qur	Qur'an
Rev	Revelation
Rom	Romans
Ruth	Ruth
1–2 Sam	1–2 Samuel
Song	Song of Songs
1–2 Tim	1–2 Timothy
Zech	Zechariah

End Notes

Introduction

Lynn Gottlieb, *She Who Dwells Within: A Feminist Vision of a Renewed Judaism* (San Francisco: Harper San Francisco, 1995), 60.

Michael Handelzalts, "Living With Contradiction: Personal reflections on the passing of a Polish philosopher," *Haaretz*, July 30, 2009, http://www.haaretz.com/living-with-contradiction-1.281107.

Elisabeth Schüssler Fiorenza, *But She Said: Feminist Practices of Biblical Interpretation* (Boston: Beacon, 1992), 54–57.

Fokkelien van Dijk-Hemmes, "Ruth: A Product of Women's Culture," in *A Feminist Companion to Ruth*, ed. Athalya Brenner (Sheffield, UK: Sheffield Academic Press, 1993), 134.

Ruth Hoppin, *Priscilla's Letter: Finding the Author of the Epistle to the Hebrews* (Fort Bragg, CA: Lost Coast, 1997).

Nurit Zarchi, "And She Is Joseph," in *Dreaming the Actual Contemporary Fiction and Poetry by Israeli Women Writers*, ed. Miriyam Glazer (Albany, NY: State University of New York Press, 2000), 19–23.

Part I: Tanakh

Eve (The first woman)

See Gen 2:20—5:4, in particular chapter 3.

1. Israeli poet T. Carmi suggests that Eve was aware of the consequences of her actions in his collection *At the Stone of Losses* (Philadelphia: Jewish Publication Society of America, 1983), 8–9.

5. Gen 1:4 "And God saw the light, that it was good" (KJV), see also Gen 1:12, 18, 21, 25.

6–7. Gen 1:5 "And there was evening, and there was morning – the first day" (NIV), see also Gen 1:8, 13, 19, 23, 31.

End Notes

8. The seventh day was the day of perfection when God rested after creation.

10. Gen 3:6.

11. Gen 2:19–20, 3:20.

12. Gen 3:24, a sword guards the garden entrance.

14. Gen 3:15, the serpent-tempter.

18–21. Gen 3:20.

22. Gen 3:21.

23. Gen 3:18 "It will produce thorns and thistles for you" (NIV).

24–25. Gen 2:15, here Eve is cast as the capable caretaker.

26. Gen 3:8.

Raouda (Ruth)

See Ruth 1:1—4:22.

Raouda is an Arabic name; the substitution serves as a reminder of Ruth's heritage in Moab (modern-day Jordan).

1. Mo'ab (موآب) is the name of Ruth's homeland in Arabic; in Modern Hebrew pronunciation it is rendered Mo'av (מוֹאָב).

2. Poet Shulamit Kalugai imagines Ruth remembering her Moabite past with her grandson in "Somewhere" (Ei-sham) in Wendy I. Zierler, *And Rachel Stole the Idols: The Emergence of Modern Hebrew Women's Writing* (Detroit: Wayne State University Press, 2004), 47. Ruth's grandson is Jesse, the father of King David.

8. Ruth 4:17, Obed, son of Ruth and Boaz.

12. Madaba is located in an area near the Jordan River and Dead Sea, which floods seasonally.

14. The name Boaz (בֹּעַז) means "swiftness." See "The NAS Old Testament Hebrew Lexicon: Bo'az," http://www.biblestudytools.com/lexicons/hebrew/nas/boaz.html. In Arabic, the word *baz* (باز) means "falcon" or "hawk." See "Bāz," *Oxford Dictionaries* (Oxford: Oxford University Press, 2014). The BDB Hebrew and English Lexicon notes the possible connection to Arabic with common elements in Bo'az and *ba'azn* (بَعْز). See Francis Brown, Samuel Rolles Driver and Charles Augustus Briggs, *A Hebrew and English*

End Notes

Lexicon of the Old Testament with an appendix containing the Biblical Aramaic (Oxford: Clarendon, 1906), 126.

Vashti (Queen of Persia)

See Esth 1:1–21.

3. Esth 1:10–11.

6–7. Esth 1:11 "... in order to display her beauty to the people and nobles, for she was lovely to look at" (NIV).

8. Some commentaries suggest that Vashti was called upon to appear naked before the king's drunken guests. See Sidnie White Crawford, "Esther," in *Eerdmans Commentary on the Bible*, eds. James D. G. Dunn and J. W. Rogerson (Grand Rapids, MI: W.B. Eerdmans, 2003), 330.

9. The Targum derives the meaning for Esther from the Persian word for star, *setareh* (ستاره) which may be a reference to the king's title of "morning star of the throne." See Paulus Cassel, *An Explanatory Commentary on Esther: With Four Appendices Consisting of the Second Targum Translated from the Aramaic with Notes* (Edinburgh: T. & T. Clark, 1888), 55. Stars are an important symbol for the Jewish people as well as in Islamic and Zoroastrian traditions.

14–16. Esth 1:12–18.

38. Esth 2:1–2 "Let a search be made for beautiful young virgins for the king" (NIV).

44–45. We do not know Vashti's fate. In Esth 1:19, "Vashti is never again to come before King Ahasuerus" (ESV).

49–50. Traditional midrash suggests Queen Vashti was vain and wicked. Rabbis even argued her refusal to appear resulted from leprosy rather than modesty. Some went so far as to write that angel Gabriel had given Vashti a tail. See Jo Carruthers, *Esther Through the Centuries* (Malden, MA: Blackwell, 2008), 61–89.

Nebiyah (The prophetess who bore Isaiah's children)

See Isa 8:1–4.

End Notes

Nebiyah (נְבִיאָה) is the female form of the Hebrew word for prophet. See Jack Hayford, *Holy Bible New Spirit-Filled Life Bible, New Living Translation; Kingdom Equipping Through the Power of the Word,* (Nashville, TN: Thomas Nelson Inc, 2013), 337. This word is the only name provided in the text for the mother of Isaiah's children.

1–3. Isa 1:2.

6–7. Isa 7:3, 8:3.

8. Isa 6:6–7.

12–17. Isa 7:14, note that the verse is typically translated "the *virgin* will conceive and give birth . . ." (NIV) but the word *'almah* (עַלְמָה) is more accurately rendered "young woman," which may suggest that this text is not only prophesy but also reports an event from Isaiah's lifetime. See Norman K. Gottwald, "Immanuel as the Prophet's Son," *Vetus Testamentum.* 8 (1) (1958) 36–47; and Craig A. Evans, *To See and Not Perceive: Isaiah 6.9–10 in Early Jewish and Christian Interpretation* (Sheffield, UK: Journal for the Study of the Old Testament, 1989), 38.

19–21. Isa 8:1 ". . . Take a large scroll, and write on it with a man's pen" (NKJV).

24. The names of Isaiah's sons mean "a remnant will return" (7:3) and "quick to the plunder" (Isa 8:3). See Warren W. Wiersbe, *The Bible Exposition Commentary: Prophets* (Wheaton, Ill: Victor Books, 1989), 10.

27. Isa 6:2–4.

28. Isa 6:8.

29. Allusion to Gomer, the prophet Hosea's wife in the book of Hosea.

31. Hos 1:6, Hosea's daughter Lo-Ruhumah.

32. Hos 1:8–9, Hosea's son Lo-Ammi.

33. Hab 1:2; Ps 6:3, 13:1, 35:17, 89:46.

37. Readers and scholars alike often assume that Isaiah and the mother of his children were married, but this notion is never confirmed in scripture.

38–40. Isa 40:31.

42. The name Immanuel (Isa 7:14) means "God is with us." See Matt 1:23.

44. Isa 40:31 "but those who hope in the Lord will renew their strength" (NIV).

End Notes

Hajar (Hagar)

See Gen 16:1–16, 21:8–21, 25:12–18; Gal 4:21–31.

Hajar is the Arabic version of the name Hagar.

1. Gen 16:1.

6. Gen 16:7, 21:15.

7. Hajar's name means to flee, wander, emigrate, and bears synergies in Arabic with the root *hajj* (حج) meaning pilgrim and pilgrimage. See Herbert Lockyer, *All the Women of the Bible: The Life and Times of All the Women of the Bible* (Grand Rapids, MI: Zondervan, 1967), 61.

19–20. Gen 12:10–13:2.

22. Gen 16:4 ". . . she looked with contempt on her mistress" (ESV).

24. Gen 18:4.

26. Gen 16:6 "Then Sarai mistreated Hagar; so she fled from her" (NIV).

27. In Islamic tradition, Hajar ran between two hills searching for water.

31. Gen 26:4 "I will make your descendants as numerous as the stars in the sky" (NIV).

32. Gen 18:12 "So Sarah laughed to herself . . ." (NIV).

41. John 13:5.

42. 2 Sam 13:10 ". . . so I may eat from your hand" (NIV).

46–48. Gen 16:13 "She gave this name to the Lord who spoke to her: "You are the God who sees me" (NIV).

Ya'el (Destroyer of Sisera)

See Judg 4:1–5:31.

Ya'el is the Hebrew transliteration of Jael or Ja'el.

1. Ya'el (יָעֵל) means "ibex." See "Ya'el: Ibex," http://biblehub.com/strongs/hebrew/3277.htm. Pitting the mountainous landscape against a small but strong mountain-climbing goat provides a useful metaphor for the power differential between Ya'el and Sisera. Mountains feature prominently in the story as Mount Tabor was used by Deborah and Barak's army to sweep down and defeat Sisera's army.

End Notes

2. Judg 4:19, 5:25.

4. Judg 4:17, "...Sisera fled away on foot to the tent of Jael" (ESV). See also Judg 5:24.

8–10. Judg 5:27.

11–12. During Rosh Hashana, one hundred shofar (ram's horn trumpet) blasts are sounded in commemoration of the number of times Sisera's mother cried for his death at the hands of the "Israelites," however Ya'el was a Kenite. See Jeffrey M. Cohen, *1,001 Questions and Answers on Rosh Hashanah and Yom Kippur* (Northvale, NJ: Jason Aronson, 1997), 237.

14. Judg 4:21, 5:26.

Jezebel (Queen of Israel)

See 1 Kgs 16:29-33, 18:1—19:18; 21:1-29; 2 Kgs 9:1-37; Rev 2:20.

1. The form of this poem is inspired by poet Lawrence Ferlinghetti's "Constantly Risking Absurdity."

2. 2 Kgs 9:30 "... and she painted her face" (KJV).

3. Lesley Hazelton argues that Jezebel's fierce defense of her god Ba'al would be a laudable action if not written by her enemies. See *Jezebel: The Untold Story of the Bible's Harlot Queen* (New York: Doubleday, 2007), 5.

4. Rev 2:20.

5. 2 Kgs 9:30 "... arranged her hair" (NIV).

6–7. 2 Kgs 9:30: Jehu.

8–10. 1 Kgs 21:1-23.

11–14. 1 Kgs 18:1-40.

15. Jezebel was a Phoenician princess (1 Kgs 16:31); her father was the king of Tyre, a city which was prophesied to be thrown into the sea (Zech 9:3-4).

16. Jezebel's name as it appears in scripture is suspected to be a demeaning epithet bestowed on the foreign ruler by the writer. See Hazleton, *Jezebel*, 2.

17. 2 Kgs 9:36.

24. 2 Kgs 9:30 "... looked out of a window" (NIV).

28. 2 Sam 5:11.

End Notes

Jephthah's Daughter (The sacrifice)

See Judg 11:1–40.

Jephthah's daughter's name is not given because, as Mieke Bal writes, "the text denies her name," in *Death & Dissymetry: The Politics of Coherence in the Book of Judges* (Chicago: The University of Chicago Press, 1988), 43.

1. Judg 11:39–40.

3–4. Judg 11:37.

8. Judg 11:35 "for I have opened my mouth unto the Lord, and I cannot go back" (KJV).

19. Ps 121:1 "I will lift up my eyes to the hills —From whence comes my help" (NKJV).

21. Gen 22:1–19, Isaac is saved from sacrifice.

22. Qur 37:102, In Islamic tradition, Ishmael is the son of Abraham saved from sacrifice.

23. Dan 3:14–30, exiles Shadrach, Meshach, and Abednego are saved from the furnace.

24. Gen 22:13, a ram is sacrificed in place of Isaac.

25. Gen 22:11–12.

26. Exod 3:2.

27. Dan 3:25, 28.

31. Lev 1:3, 10, 23:19; Num 7:17, 23, 29, 35, 41, 47, 53, 59, 65, 71, 77, 83, 88; Ezek 6:17, etc.

Rahab (A woman of Jericho)

See Josh 2:1–24, 6:1–27.

Rahab may not be her given name, but rather a designation derived from a word meaning "wide," or "broad," See Athalya Brenner, "Wide Gaps, Narrow Escapes: I am Known as Rahab, the Broad," in *First Person: Essays in Biblical Autobiography*, ed. Philip R. Davies (London: Sheffield Academic, 2002), 47. First century historian Josephus mentions inn-keeping in his account of Rahab, but nothing of prostitution. Josephus has no qualms about naming Delilah a harlot. See Josephus: *The Antiquities of the Jews*, Book V.

End Notes

Furthermore, Abravanel notes the misconduct of the spies as they went beyond their orders from Joshua to "Go, look over the land," in Josh 2:1 (NIV), instead visiting Rahab in the city. See Yitzhak ben Yehudah Abarbanel, *Pirush al Neviim Rishonim* [Commentary on the Early Prophets] (Jerusalem, 1960), http://www.hebrewbooks.org/pagefeed/hebrewbooks_org_14367_22.pdf.

5. Josh 6:20–21.

7–8. Josh 6:22–25.

15. The name Jericho may be related to the word *reah* (רֵיחַ) which means scent or fragrance. See Zev Vilnay, *The Sacred Land: Volume 2* (Philadelphia: Jewish Publication Society of America, 1973), 81.

18. Num 13:33.

19. Josh 6:24, 8:27.

20. Num 31:9.

22–28. Josh 2:1–6.

37. Athalya Brenner suggests the quantities of flax bales necessary to hide the two spies would be expensive, and not financially feasible possessions for someone without a hand in the textile business. See Brenner, "Wide Gaps, Narrow Escapes," 48.

40. The name Jericho may derive from the Canaanite word *yareah* (יָרֵחַ) which means "moon," possibly in deference to local lunar deities. See Jerome Murphy-O'Connor, "Jericho," in *The Oxford Essential Guide to People & Places of the Bible*, eds. Bruce Manning Metzger and Michael David Coogan (New York: Berkley Books, 2001), 126.

54. Josh 2:18–21.

66. Heb 11:31. An alternative meaning for Rahab is "welcome," from the Arabic root *rahab* (رحب).

She'erah (The builder)

See 1 Chr 7:24.

1–3. She'erah is a daughter in the tribe of Ephraim, mentioned in only one verse of the Bible.

End Notes

17. The name of the city Uzzen-She'erah (אֻזֵּן שֶׁאֱרָה) could be more literally rendered "ear of She'erah." See William Smith, Horatio B. Hackett, and Ezra Abbot, *Dr. William Smith's Dictionary of the Bible: Comprising Its Antiquities, Biography, Geography, and Natural History* (New York: Hurd and Houghton, 1872), 3366. However, this wording inspired the more poetic approach that the association with ears could suggest something of "hear She'erah." A similar word in Arabic, *adhan* (أَذَان), is used for the call to prayer from the root meaning "ear" or "to listen."

Shulamith (The beloved of Solomon)

See Song of Solomon.

The precise meaning of the name Shulamith is unclear; it may be a female form of the name Solomon and related to the Hebrew word for peace, *shalom* (שָׁלוֹם), or it could be a name derived from place, as in "a woman from Shulem" or alternatively Shunem. See "*NET Bible*," note on Song 6:13, http://net.bible.org/#!bible/Song+of+Songs.

1–6. Song 6:10.

7–8. Song 4:16.

9. Song 2:16, 6:3.

10–12. With a female first person narrator, is this a written by the king—a song *of* Solomon, or a song *to* Solomon? See Richard S. Hess, *Song of Songs* (Grand Rapids, MI: Baker Academic, 2005), 19–20.

13. Song 2:10.

14. Song 2:8, 17.

15. Song 2:11.

16. Song 7:12.

17. Song 2:1.

Miriam (The prophetess)

See Exod 2:1–9, 15:1–21; Num 12:1–16.

2. Exod 2:5–10.

3. Exod 2:1–4.

End Notes

4. Exod 15:20.

5. Exod 7:17.

6. Colin Humphreys suggests that the ten plagues in Egypt were caused by natural scientific phenomena in *The Miracles of Exodus: A Scientist's Discovery of the Extraordinary Natural Causes of the Biblical Stories* (San Francisco, CA: Harper San Francisco, 2003), 111–88.

9. Exod 14:21.

11. A wind set-down effect could displace water from even a large body such as the Red Sea. See Humphreys, *The Miracles of Exodus*, 244–62.

12–13. The *Yam Suph* (יַם־סוּף), most commonly known as the "Red Sea" may be more accurately translated "Sea of Reeds" and could refer to the Nile Delta, or a variety of other locations. See Humphreys, *The Miracles of Exodus*, 188–205.

15. Michael Coogan speculates that the entirety of the song in Exod 15 might properly belong to Miriam, not just Exod 15:20–21. See *The Old Testament: A Very Short Introduction* (Oxford: Oxford University Press, 2008), 46. In this case, she may have had more of a leadership role than is typically assigned her in scripture.

16. Exod 13:21–22.

17–18. Num 12:2, In context Miriam and Aaron's complaint against Moses seems unjust, but it is evidence that they believed, perhaps rightly so, that God did not only speak to their brother, see also Miriam's designation in Exod 15:20.

Saffūrah (Zipporah)

See Exod 2:11–22, 3:1–7, 4:25, 18:2–6.

1–2. Zipporah's name in Islamic tradition is Saffūrah. She was from Midian, likely in the area of modern day Saudi Arabia. Saffūrah cared for her father's flocks (Exod 2:16).

7. Zipporah's Hebrew name may stem from the Hebrew word for bird, *tsippor* (צִפּוֹר) while Saffūrah is closely related to an Arabic word for bird, 'asaffūr (عصفور).

8. Alternatively, her name may be related to the word *tsefirah* (צְפִירָה) "diadem" in Isa 28:5. See Mitchell Joseph Dahood, "Eblaite and Biblical Hebrew," *The Catholic Biblical Quarterly* 44 (1982) 7.

9–12. Exod 3:1–8, some scientists offer natural explanations for the burning bush, such as a volcanic vent. See Humphreys, *The Miracles of Exodus*, 61–88.

34–35. Saffūrah's name also could be related to the word for viper (צֶפַע) in Isa 14:29, and/or *çaparu* in Assyrian (howling). See W. Muss-Arnolt, *A Concise Dictionary of the Assyrian Languages* (Berlin: Reuther & Reichard, 1905), 885.

Khuldah (Huldah)

See 2 Kgs 22:14–20; 2 Chr 34:22–28.

Huldah's name is respelled to reflect Modern Hebrew pronunciation in which the letter Het (ח) has merged with Khaf (כ) to create a voiceless uvular fricative.

1. Deut 29:20.

2–5. There are two sets of now blocked gates in Jerusalem named "The Huldah Gates." These could have been named after the prophetess for the place where she held court and might have been buried. Or the name could be a reference to the tunnels leading up from the gates, similar to those used by burrowing rodents, as one possible meaning for Huldah (חֻלְדָּה) is "mole." See Tikva S. Frymer, S. David Sperling, and Aaron Rothkoff, "Huldah." In *Encyclopaedia Judaica: 2nd ed. Vol. 9*, eds. Michael Berenbaum and Fred Skolnik. (Detroit: Macmillan Reference USA, 2007), 580–581, and Katharina Galor and Hanswulf Bloedhorn, *The Archaeology of Jerusalem: From the Origins to the Ottomans* (New Haven: Yale University Press, 2013), 81–82.

9–11. 2 Kgs 22:16 (ESV).

12. 2 Chr 29:6 (NIV).

14–15. 2 Kgs 22:17 (ESV).

16–22. Ibid.

23–25. 2 Kgs 22:19 (NASB).

26–29. 2 Kgs 22:20 (ESV).

End Notes

30. Num 14:18.

31–32. This is a traditional liturgical script for the scripture reader just following a Biblical passage and its congregational response. See Church of England, *Common Worship: Services and Prayers for the Church of England, Pastoral Services* (London: Church House, 2000), 33.

Dabourah (Deborah)

See Judg 4:1–5:31.

Dabourah's name is Arabicized as a reminder she was likely from an area in modern-day Palestine.

1–2. Judg 4:4, Dabourah is known as "wife of Lapidoth," which may mean not that she is married to a man named Lapidoth whose name means "torches," but rather suggests that she is a "fiery woman," a force to be reckoned with, as evidenced by her actions in Judges. See Cheryl Anne Brown, *No Longer Be Silent: First Century Jewish Portraits of Biblical Women: Studies in Pseudo-Philo's Biblical Antiquities and Josephus's Jewish Antiquities* (Louisville, KY: Westminster J. Knox, 1992), 43.

3. The common translation for the name Deborah is "bee," which might allude to domestic qualities of efficiency and productivity, but her name also might also translate to "wasp" or "hornet," the stronger meaning lost in traditional translations. (The word *daboor* دبور means "wasp" in Arabic). See Judith R. Baskin, *Jewish Women in Historical Perspective* (Detroit: Wayne State University Press, 1991), 90.

5. Judg 4:4.

6–8. Judg 4:5, "She held court under the Palm of Deborah. . ." (NIV).

9–11. Judg 4:6.

12–14. Judg 4:8–9.

15–16. Judg 4:14.

17–19. Judg 4:17, Ya'el's name means "ibex." See "Ya'el: Ibex," http://biblehub.com/strongs/hebrew/3277.htm.

22. Judg 5:1–31.

End Notes

Hannah (The mother of Samuel)

See 1 Sam 1:1–2:11.

1. 1 Sam 1:3.

3. 1 Sam 2:19.

6. 1 Sam 1:7, 10.

7. 1 Sam 1:13.

15. 1 Sam 1:12.

16. This line imagines the priest's trajectory similarly to the way Emily Dickinson envisions the fly in the poem "I heard a Fly buzz — when I died —" (591). See Emily Dickinson, *The Poems of Emily Dickinson* (Cambridge, MA: Belknap, 1998), 265–6.

19–20. 1 Sam 1:14.

26. 1 Sam 1:15.

28. 1 Sam 1:16.

31. 1 Sam 1:24.

33–35. 1 Sam 1:17.

38–41. 1 Sam 1:11.

42. 1 Sam 1:20.

Malikah (Queen of Sheba)

See 1 Kgs 10:1–13.

The Queen of Sheba is only referred to in Judaic scripture by her title and country. Islamic tradition names her Bilqis. Taking a middle path, the queen's name here is Malikah (ملكة), the Arabic word for queen, a nod to the tradition that she might hail from Yemen.

2. 1 Kgs 3:10–12, 10:1.

9. Matt 12:42.

10. Sheba may have been in the region which is modern day Yemen. See Jamal J. Elias, "Prophecy, Power and Propriety: The Encounter of Solomon and the Queen of Sheba," *Journal of Qur'anic Studies* 11 (2009) 57–74.

11. Ethiopian tradition claims the Queen of Sheba as a queen of Ethiopia. See Alice Ogden Bellis, "The Queen of Sheba: A Gender-Sensitive Reading," *The Journal of Religious Thought* 51 (1994) 22–23.

12. Some Islamic traditions assert the Queen of Sheba was of the djinn. See Jacob Lassner, *Demonizing the Queen of Sheba: Boundaries of Gender and Culture in Postbiblical Judaism and Medieval Islam* (Chicago: University of Chicago Press, 1993), 208.

Bathsheba (The mother of Solomon)

See 2 Sam 11:1—12:25; 1 Kgs 1:1–53.

1. 1 Chr 3:5.

5. The root verb *shaba* (שבה) means "to take captive." See A. F. Kirkpatrick, *The Book of Psalms*: Books II and III (Cambridge, UK: Cambridge University Press, 1902), 304.

6. The root verb *shama'* (שמע) means "to hear," as in Deut 6:3, "Sh'ma Yisra'el." See Eugene E. Carpenter and Philip Wesley Comfort, *Holman Treasury of Key Bible Words: 200 Greek and 200 Hebrew Words Defined and Explained* (Nashville, TN: Holman Reference, 2000), 83.

7. The root verb *natan* (נתן) means "to give." See James Strong, *Strong's Exhaustive Concordance of the Bible* (Peabody, MA: Hendrickson, 2007), 1543.

8. The meaning of the name Solomon is often translated "peace," but the root *shalem* (שָׁלֵם) means to be whole or unbroken. See Heinrich Gross, "Peace," in *Encyclopedia of Biblical Theology*, ed. Johannes B. Bauer (New York: Crossroad, 1981), 648.

12. Ps 51:1.

13. 1 Kgs 4:30–32.

16. Ps 51:2.

19. Job 16:12.

23. Isa 30:14.

25. Jer 36:23.

29–30. Isa 58:12.

END NOTES

31. Prov 8:33, 19:20. Many commentators agree that "King Lemuel" of Proverbs 31 is actually Solomon. See D. W. Gooding, "The Septuagint's Version of Solomon's Misconduct," *Vetus Testamentum* 15, no. 3 (1965) 328. If this is the case, the sayings Lemuel's mother taught him (Prov 31:1) were from Solomon's mother, Bathsheba.

32. Prov 2:1–5.

34. Prov 3:3.

38. Prov 31:10, "woman of valor" (אֵשֶׁת חַיִל). See Ronald L. Eisenberg, *The JPS Guide to Jewish Traditions* (Philadelphia: Jewish Publication Society, 2004), 129.

42. 2 Sam 11:4.

Sahrai (Sarah)

See Gen 18:1–15.

Sarah's name here is a variation on her birth name Sarai (שָׂרַי). God renames Sarai in Gen 17:15, but does this when appearing to her husband, Abraham.

1. Gen 18:12–13, Phyllis Trible notes that God did not ask Sarah why she laughed, but Abraham. See *Hagar, Sarah, and Their Children: Jewish, Christian, and Muslim Perspectives* (Louisville, KY: Westminster John Knox, 2006), 43.

2–3. Gen 17:1–22.

11. Gen 17:17–18.

14. Terrence Fretheim argues that the question might not be an accusation or reprimand, but rather a positive attempt to continue the conversation. No judgment is made on Sarah for laughing at God. See *Abraham: Trials of Family and Faith*, (Columbia, SC: University of South Carolina Press, 2007), 113–4.

15–16. Gen 18:14.

33. Gen 18:15, Fretheim continues with the idea that God gives Sarah permission to laugh, letting her know the laughter will be transformed in time. See Fretheim, *Abraham*, 114–5.

End Notes

Rebeqah (Rebecca)

See Gen 24:1–67, 25:19—27:46.

The alternative spelling renders the *qof* (ק) in Rebecca's name from Hebrew (רִבְקָה).

1. Carol Meyers notes the unusual agency Rebeqah demonstrates in her narrative. See Carol Meyers, "Rebekah," in *Women in Scripture: A Dictionary of Named and Unnamed Women in the Hebrew Bible, the Apocryphal/Deuterocanonical Books, and the New Testament*, eds. Carol Meyers, Toni Craven, and Ross S. Kraemer (Boston: Houghton Mifflin, 2000), 143–4.

4. Gen 24:18.

8–9. Gen 24:8.

10–12. Gen 24:14.

13–17. Gen 24:20.

18. Gen 25:20.

19–21. Gen 24:29–30.

24. Gen 24:61.

28. Gen 24:63.

29. Gen 24:67.

30–32. Gen 25:22–23.

Rahela (Rachel)

See Gen 29:1—33:20, 35:16–24.

Rahela is an imagined diminutive form of Rachel (רָחֵל).

1–2. *Henry IV*, Part 1, Act 2, Scene 2.

5. See Wendy I. Zierler, *And Rachel Stole the Idols: The Emergence of Modern Hebrew Women's Writing* (Detroit: Wayne State University Press, 2004), 3.

6–10. Gen 31:35.

11. Zierler, *And Rachel Stole the Idols*, 4.

12. Gen 24:29, 53, 29:27, Rachel's father Laban repeatedly profits from the marriages of the females of his household.

END NOTES

17. Gen 30:15.

18. Gen 31:33, Rom 3:12.

19. Gen 31:34.

20. Gen 31:35.

27. Gen 31:32, Jacob says, ". . . if you find anyone who has your gods, that person shall not live" (NIV).

33. Gen 29:26.

34. Gen 30:34–43.

35. Gen 35:18.

Joseph (The first child of Jacob and Rachel)

See Gen 30:22–24, 37:1–36, 39:1—50:26.

1–2. Israeli writer Nurit Zarchi wrote a short story and poem elaborating on this thought. See "And She Is Joseph," 19–23, and "She Is Joseph," in *The Defiant Muse: Hebrew Feminist Poems from Antiquity to the Present, a Bilingual Anthology*, eds. Shirley Kaufman, Galit Hasan-Rokem, and Tamar S. Hess (London: Loki Books, 2000), 167.

11. Gen 30:24. See Joel T. Klein, *Through the Name of God: A New Road to the Origin of Judaism and Christianity* (Westport, CT: Greenwood, 2001), 17.

12–13. Gen 35:18, The meanings of "Ben-Oni," the name Rachel gave her second son, and "Benjamin," the name Jacob gave him. See David Noel Freedman, Allen C. Myers, and Astrid B. Beck, eds., *Eerdmans Dictionary of the Bible* (Grand Rapids, MI: Eerdmans, 2000), 166.

26. Gen 29:17.

27. Gen 39:6 "And Joseph was of beautiful form, and fair to look upon" (JPS).

28–29. Gen 37:3, The "coat of many colors" phrase *ketonet passim* (כְּתֹנֶת פַּסִּים) which might actually mean "coat with long sleeves" or even "coat of distinction," is exactly the same words as those used for the garment of King David's daughter Tamar. In 2 Sam 13:18–19, the text specifically mentions this as a type of clothing worn by virgin daughters of the king,

End Notes

the only other time this phrase appears in scripture besides the reference to Joseph's coat.

30. Gen 37:28–36.

31. Gen 39:1–20.

32–33. Gen 48:5.

34–35. Gen 49:25 (ESV).

37. Gen 49:22 (JPS).

38–39. Gen 50:23 (NASB).

40–41. Another example of birth "on the knees" of someone is the following: Gen 30:3 "And she said, Behold my maid Bilhah, go in unto her; and she shall bear upon my knees, that I may also have children by her" (KJV). See Hebrew Interlinear Bible, "Genesis 30," http://www.scripture4all.org/OnlineInterlinear/OTpdf/gen30.pdf.

42. Gen 41:45, Joseph's new name from Pharaoh (צָפְנַת פַּעְנֵחַ).

44. The etymology of Zaphnath-paaneah is unclear, but the name may mean "revealer of secrets." See A. Kenneth Abraham and Matthew Henry, eds., *Matthew Henry Study Bible: King James Version* (Peabody, MA: Hendrickson Bibles, 2010), 87.

45. Gen 3/:5.

Shekinah (God)

1. Job 33:4.

2. The Hebrew gender of the word for spirit, *ruaḥ* (רוּחַ), is feminine. See "Job 33," http://www.scripture4all.org/OnlineInterlinear/OTpdf/job33.pdf.

4–6. The Hebrew root *shadad* (שָׁדַד) means "to destroy," but the meaning of El Shaddai may be closer to a related Arabic word which means "strong," *shadiid* (شديد). See "Shadad," http://www.blueletterbible.org/lang/lexicon/Lexicon.cfm?Strongs=H7703&t=KJV.

7. *Ehyeh asher ehyeh* (אֶהְיֶה אֲשֶׁר אֶהְיֶה) means "I AM WHO I AM" in Hebrew.

11. Isa 42:14 ". . . like a woman in childbirth, I cry out, I gasp and pant" (NIV).

12. Deut 32:18 (ESV).

13. Isa 49:15.

14. Isa 66:13.

18. Ps 113:5.

19. Hos 11:3–4.

20. Deut 32:11–12 (KJV).

21. Luke 15:8–10.

Noadiah (The prophetess)

See Neh 6:1–19.

Noadiah's name can be rendered "Yahweh has met by appointment." See Geoffrey W. Bromiley et al., eds., *The International Standard Bible Encyclopedia. Volume 3: K-P* (Grand Rapids, MI: Eerdmans, 1988), 543. Thanks to Norman Yeung for inspiring Noadiah's street artist persona.

1. In Neh 6:15, the text indicates the walls and gates were rebuilt in fifty-two days, however Josephus writes that the city walls took two years four months to build. See Josephus, "Antiquities of the Jews," Book 11, Chapter 5, Paragraph 8. See "Antiquities of the Jews - Book XI," http://www.earlyjewishwritings.com/text/josephus/ant11.html.

Some scholars mention that the local opposition to Nehemiah's wall building may have been well-founded given the wall's implications for relations with neighbors. See Robert Carroll, "Coopting the Prophets: Nehemiah and Noadiah," in *Priests, Prophets, and Scribes: Essays on the Formation and Heritage of Second Temple Judaism in Honour of Joseph Blenkinsopp*, eds. Joseph Blenkinsopp and Eugene Charles Ulrich (Sheffield, UK: Journal for the Study of the Old Testament, 1992), 95.

Irit (The wife of Lot)

See Gen 19:1–29; Luke 17:28–33.

Lot's wife is given no name by scripture. A midrashic name for her is Irit. See Rebecca Goldstein, "Looking Back at Lot's Wife," in *Out of the Garden: Women Writers on the Bible*, eds. Christina Büchmann and Celina Spiegel (New York: Fawcett Columbine, 1994), 3–12. Another name for her is Idit, which shares letters with the Hebrew word for witness. See Sharon Cohen

End Notes

Anisfeld, Tara Mohr, and Catherine Spector, eds., *The Women's Passover Companion: Women's Reflections on the Festival of Freedom* (Woodstock, VT: Jewish Lights, 2003) 78–98, 269. In Arabic the phrase *ya reit* (ياريت) means "I wish."

1–2. Ramban (Nachmanides) argued that Lot's wife acted from a protective impulse, to see if someone was following them out of the city. See Moses Nachmanides, *Commentary on the Torah Vol. 1 Bereshit / Genesis* (Brooklyn, NY: Shilo, 1973), 261.

3. Gen 19:24.

4. Gen 19:19, Lot says to the angels, "But I can't flee to the mountains; this disaster will overtake me, and I'll die" (NIV).

7. Luke 17:31.

9–10. Gen 19:29.

11–12. Gen 3:6.

21–25. Gen 19:3–8.

26. There is a rock formation on the Jordan side of the Dead Sea known as the "Lot's wife" pillar. See James L. Kugel, *How to Read the Bible: A Guide to Scripture, Then and Now* (New York: Free, 2007), 130. Perhaps it was there before Lot and his family escaped.

30–32. Gen 19:17.

38. Gen 19:16.

40–41. Gen 19:26.

46. Gen 19:26. According to scripture, Lot's wife turned into a pillar of salt, but given the value of salt at the time, it could understood that she turned into a pillar of gold. In some parts of the world salt was even used as currency. Ethiopia used *amole tchew* (salt blocks) until the end of the 19th century. See "Salt blocks used as currency," http://www.bbc.co.uk/ahistoryoftheworld/objects/vDn91YroQr-CC4OpxxEtDw.

47–49. Luke 17:33.

50. Luke 17:34.

54–55. Gen 19:27–28.

End Notes

Yidana (The witch of Endor)

See 1 Sam 28:3–25.

As the "Witch of Endor" was given no name in scripture, her name here is an invented variation on a word for mediums or those "with a familiar spirit" in Hebrew, *yiddeoni* (יִדְּעֹנִי) (JPS). See Strong, *Strong's Exhaustive Concordance of the Bible*, 1506.

2. 1 Sam 28:3.

42. 1 Sam 28:5, Azrael is a traditional name for the Angel of Death.

43. 1 Sam 28:11.

Tamar (The three)

See Gen 38:1–28; 2 Sam 13:1–32, 14:27; 1 Chr 2:4, 3:9.

1. The name Tamar (תָּמָר) means "date palm." See T. K. Cheyne and J. Sutherland Black, eds. *Encyclopedia Biblica: A Critical Dictionary of the Literary, Political and Religious History, the Archaeology, Geography, and Natural History of the Bible* (New York: Macmillan Co, 1899), 4891.

2. Tamarind is a legumous fruit-bearing tree that grows in Africa, Arabia, and Southeast Asia.

3. The Tamarisk tree appears in both the Bible (*eshel*, אֶשֶׁל) in Gen 21:33 and 1 Sam 22:6; and the Qur'an, Qur 34:16 (*'aathl* أثل). See Cheyne and Black, *Encyclopedia Biblica*, 4892.

17–24. Gen 38:6–30.

25–26. The twins of Tamar (and Judah) were named Zerah "rising up," and Perez "breaking through." See Strong, *Strong's Exhaustive Concordance of the Bible*, 1494, 1561.

27. 2 Sam 13:1–21.

28. "Salt cedar" is another name for the Tamarisk tree. See James A. Duke, Peggy-Ann K. Duke and Judith L. DuCellier, *Duke's Handbook of Medicinal Plants of the Bible* (Boca Raton, FL: CRC, 2008), 451.

30–35. Phyllis Trible's *Texts of Terror* points out that Tamar was able to remain calm in trying to use wisdom and reason with her attacker, (Philadelphia: Fortress, 1984), 45.

End Notes

36. 2 Sam 14:27, Absalom's daughter Tamar is perhaps named after her aunt, Absalom's sister.

41. Gen 14:7 and 2 Chr 20:2 mention Hazezon, a city in the region Tamar.

42. Mazandaran and Yazd provinces in modern Iran both have villages with names similar to Tamar (تمر and طامهر).

Delilah (The beloved of Samson)

See Judg 16:1–22.

1. Judg 16:13–14, The name Delilah could be related to the noun *dallah* (דַּלָּה) which means "lock of hair," or "braid" See "Delilah," http://www.abarim-publications.com/Meaning/Delilah.html.

2. Judg 16:7–9 (NIV).

3. Judg 16:3.

4. The name Delilah may come from the root *dalal* (דָּלַל) which means "to hang low." See "Dalal," http://biblehub.com/hebrew/1809.htm.

5. Judg 16:5.

7. The root *dalal* is also used by Isaiah to describe a river bed (Isa 19:6). See "Isaiah 19," http://scripture4all.org/OnlineInterlinear/OTpdf/isa19.pdf.

9. Judg 15:4.

11. Judg 16:17.

14. Judg 14:12.

15. Judg 14:16–17, 16:17.

21. The "Delilah" tweet from the Twitter account @YesAllBiblicalWomen prompted this question about Delilah's motives which doxa typically assumes to be money lust. See "Delilah: June 4, 2014," http://twitter.com/AllBibleWomen/status/474354952664412161.

22–25. Judg 16:5.

26. Judg 16:21.

Peninnah (Wife of Elkanah)

See 1 Sam 1:1–5.

End Notes

1–15. Scholar Lillian Klein asserts that Peninnah is probably a fictional stock character, evidenced by her lack of dialogue and independent actions in the scriptural narrative, set up by the author to be a literary foil for the childless heroine, Hannah. See Lillian R. Klein, "Peninnah," in *Women in Scripture: A Dictionary of Named and Unnamed Women in the Hebrew Bible, the Apocryphal/Deuterocanonical Books, and the New Testament*, eds. Carol Meyers, Toni Craven, and Ross S. Kraemer (Boston: Houghton Mifflin, 2000), 134.

20–21. 1 Sam 1:1–5.

23. Gen 29:32—30:1.

24. An allusion to the meaning of Peninnah's name (coral, פְּנִנָּה) See Klein, "Peninnah," 134.

26. Hannah speaks up to defend herself in 1 Sam 1:15; this line suggests that Peninnah's approach did not require words.

Women of the Decalogue (Women at Sinai)

See Exod 19:1–25.

1–4. Exod 19:15, "And he said to the people, 'Be ready for the third day; do not go near a woman'" (ESV).

6. Exod 19:20.

11. "... unsex me here," is spoken by Lady Macbeth in *Macbeth,* Act I, Scene 5.

13–14. Gen 1:27–31.

26. Gen 16:7–8, 21:17.

27. Gen 18:15.

28. Gen 25:23.

37–38. Elaine Goodfriend asks the question if the commandment revelation actually meant for both genders in "Yitro 18:1–20:23," in *The Torah: a women's commentary*, eds. Tamara Cohn Eskenazi and Andrea L. Weiss (New York: Women of Reform Judaism, Federation of Temple Sisterhood, 2008), 407.

End Notes

Serakh bat Asher (Daughter of Jacob's son Asher)

See Gen 46:17; Num 26:46; 1 Chr 7:30.

3. Gen 46:17; Num 26:46; 1 Chr 7:30, Serakh bat Asher's name appears before the journey to Egypt during famine, and when Moses leads the Israelites out of Egypt generations later.

9–12. 2 Sam 20:14–22, Rashi's commentary suggests Serakh bat Asher is the "Wise Woman of Abel" who prevents widespread bloodshed by finding a traitor in the city and securing his demise. See "2 Samuel 20:19," http://www.chabad.org/library/bible_cdo/aid/15880#showrashi=true.

13. Gen 30:9–13, Asher is the son of Jacob and Zilpah.

14. "I am the voice of history," Ellen Frankel suggests that Serakh's remarkably long life would have made her a natural historian of the Jewish people. See *The Five Books of Miriam: A Woman's Commentary on the Torah* (New York: G.P. Putnam's, 1996), xx.

29–30. From Exod 3:16 (פָּקֹד פָּקַדְתִּי), "I have surely remembered you" (JPS). It should be noted that the verb used here additionally connotes visiting and attending with the implication of taking action, rather than simply thinking about the subject. Thanks to Sarah Baker for this insight. The verb *pakod* (פָּקֹד) also appears with positive actions in Gen 21:1, 50:24; Ruth 1:6; and punitively in Jer 8:12, 10:15. See J. D. Douglas and Merrill C. Tenney, *Zondervan Illustrated Bible Dictionary* (Grand Rapids, MI: Zondervan, 2011), 1513.

Part II: New Testament

Kalima (The Syro-Phoenician woman)

See Matt 15:21–28; Mark 7:24–30.

Kalima (كلمة) is an Arabic name meaning "word" or "speaker," fitting for woman from what would become modern-day Syria and Lebanon who speaks back to the Son of God, possibly slyly calling Him out for His words.

7. See Rev. Vladimir Korotkov's sermon, "Was Jesus influenced by his Culture," September 13, 2009, St. Aiden Uniting Church, North Balwyn, Austalia, http://northbalwynunitingchurch.org.au/wp-content/uploads/2009_serm38.pdf.

15. Matt 15:26; Mark 7:27.

16–17. In both traditional Judaism and Islam, dogs are often considered abhorrent. See Sophia Menache, "Dogs: God's Worst Enemies?," *Society & Animals* 5 (1997) 23–44. However, Bedouins raised saluki dogs, an exception to negative cultural ideas in the Middle East regarding canines. See Jenny Berglund, "Princely Companion or Object of Offense? The Dog's Ambiguous Status in Islam," *Society & Animals* 22 (2014) 545–9.

25. See Wil Gafney's analysis, "Drag Queens and Did Jesus Just Call that Woman a B—?," last modified September 12, 2012, http://www.wilgafney.com/2012/09/12/drag-queens-and-did-jesus-just-call-that-woman-a-b.

28. Matt 15:28; Mark 7:29.

32. Matt 15:26; Mark 7:27.

Shahar (The woman accused of adultery)

See John 8:2–11.

Shahar (שַׁחַר) is a Hebrew name which means "dawn." John 8:2 mentions that Jesus was teaching at dawn in the temple courts when the woman accused of adultery was brought before Him.

3. Before this incident, John 8:1 records that Jesus had just been at the Mount of Olives.

7–8. For a woman to be "caught" in adultery, there would have to be eyewitnesses. In which case, how were the scribes and Pharisees, her accusers, present to witness this woman's sin?

11–12. John 8:5.

15–16. John 8:8.

17. John 8:9, one possibility for what Jesus wrote in the dust.

22–23. John 8:10.

25. John 8:11.

Maryam an-Nasiri (Mary, mother of Jesus)

See Matt 1:1—2:23; Luke 1:1—2:40.

End Notes

Mary's name and village are translated into Arabic as in modern times the population of Nazareth is predominately Arab.

2. Luke 1:31.

4. Luke 1:27.

5–8. Luke 1:39.

11–12. Luke 1:38.

21–22. Luke 1:36, 40–45.

23, 26. Luke 1:18–21.

28. Luke 2:7.

29. Luke 2:22.

Anna (The prophetess)

See Luke 2:36–38.

1. Luke 2:25 (KJV).

3. Anna's name comes from the Hebrew "Hannah" (חַנָּה) and means "grace."

4. Luke 2:29–32 records Simeon's words, but no specific blessings of Anna are preserved.

6, 8. Luke 2:24.

12–14. Luke 2:29–32.

15. Luke 2:32.

16. Luke 2:33–34 (NIV).

17. Male/female pairs feature prominently in the miraculous birth stories, i.e. Elizabeth/Zechariah, Mary/Joseph. See Vasiliki Limberis, "Anna 2" in *Women in Scripture: A Dictionary of Named and Unnamed Women in the Hebrew Bible, the Apocryphal/Deuterocanonical Books, and the New Testament*, eds. Carol Meyers, Toni Craven, and Ross S. Kraemer (Boston: Houghton Mifflin, 2000), 51.

18–19. Luke 2:30.

30–33. 1 Tim. 4:7.

End Notes

Salome (The dancer)

See Matt 14:1–11; Mark 6:17–28, 15:40, 16:1.

5. Mark 15:34, in Aramaic: "My God, my God, why have you forsaken me?"

9–15. Matt 14:6–8; Mark 6:22–28.

18–19. Matt 14:8–9; Mark 6:23–24.

21. Matt 14:8–10; Mark 6:24.

22. In Gustave Flaubert's "Hérodias" from *Three Tales*, Salome forgets the name of John the Baptist as she asks for his head. See Gustave Flaubert, *Three Tales*, trans. Arthur McDowall (New York: New Directions, 1959), 122.

31. Mark 15:40, 16:1.

Junia (The apostle)

See Rom 16:7.

3. In many Bible translations, the common Latin female name "Junia" (Ἰουνία) has been erroneously re-written as masculine "Junias," which does not appear in any other ancient documents. See Bernadette J. Brooten, "Junia," in *Women in Scripture: A Dictionary of Named and Unnamed Women in the Hebrew Bible, the Apocryphal/Deuterocanonical Books, and the New Testament*, eds. Carol Meyers, Toni Craven, and Ross S. Kraemer (Boston: Houghton Mifflin, 2000), 107.

4–5. Rev 22:18; Prov 30:5–6.

8–9. Junia's very existence as an apostle is often completely overlooked by the church.

11–12. Rev 22:19.

15–16. In Rom 16:7, Paul notes that Junia and Andronicus "were in Christ before me" (ESV).

Samara (The Samaritan woman)

See John 4:4–42.

End Notes

The name Samara is a nod to the woman's Samaritan heritage (modern Palestine).

1–2. John 4:6.

4–6. John 4:16.

7–24. Shawna R. B. Atteberry suggests that the Samaritan woman might have been trapped in a Levirate marriage, a widow obligated to successively marry the brothers of her husband(s). See "The Samaritan Woman," last modified March 25, 2013, http://www.crivoice.org/WT-samaritan.html.

25–26. John 4:20.

27. John 4:15.

Philip's Daughters (Four women who prophesied)

See Acts 21:8–9.

2. Acts 21:8.

3. Caesarea was a coastal city in ancient Israel.

9–10. The writer of Acts both notes the ministry of these woman and represses the message thereof. See Richard I. Pervo, "Four Unmarried Daughters of Philip," in *Women in Scripture: A Dictionary of Named and Unnamed Women in the Hebrew Bible, the Apocryphal/Deuterocanonical Books, and the New Testament*, eds. Carol Meyers, Toni Craven, and Ross S. Kraemer (Boston: Houghton Mifflin, 2000), 467–8.

Nuntia (The wife of Pilate)

See Matt 27:19.

The wife of Pilate is unnamed in scripture. The word *nuntia* means "messenger" in Latin. See F. P. Leverett et. al., *A New and Copious Lexicon of the Latin Language* (Philadelphia: J. B. Lippincott, 1850), 578.

1. Matt 27:19.

2. Matt 27:24.

5. Matt 27:48.

7. John 19:34.

END NOTES

8–9. Luke 24:39.

11–14. John 1:29; Heb 9:28.

15. Matt 27:29; Mark 15:17; John 19:2.

16–18. Luke 23:26.

19. Matt 27:30.

The Maji (Wise travelers from the East)

See Matt 2:1–12.

1. Matt 2:2.

2. Matt 2:5–6; Mic 5:2.

5. Matt 2:1.

13. The name Bishakha (বিশাখা) means "star." See Mahesh Sharma, *3500 Names for Babies* (New Delhi: Diamond Pocket Books, 1999), 64.

14. Matt 2:11.

18. Luke 24:1.

20. Malekjahan (ملک جهان) literally means "queen of the world" in Farsi. See Fergus Nicoll, *Shah Jahan* (New Delhi: Viking, 2009), 26.

21. Matt 2:11.

26. Matt 27:29.

28. Ghaziyah means "female warrior" (from *ghazi* غازي). See Ira M. Lapidus, *A History of Islamic Societies* (Cambridge: Cambridge University Press, 1988), 332.

29. Matt 2:11.

37. Matt 26:7.

39–40. Matt 2:12.

42–44. Matt 2:14.

Niyyah (The woman with the alabaster jar)

See Matt 26:6–13; Mark 14:3–9; John 12:1–8.

End Notes

Niyyah (نِيَّة) is an Islamic concept regarding the intention of one's heart to do something for God. See Cyril Glassé, *The New Encyclopedia of Islam* (Lanham, MD: Rowman & Littlefield, 2008), 247.

2. The name of the village Bethany, *bayt 'anya* (بيت عنيا) may be from Aramaic words which mean "house of poverty/affliction." See Brian J. Capper, "Essene Community Houses and Jesus' Early Community," in *Jesus and Archaeology*, ed. James H. Charlesworth (Grand Rapids, MI: Eerdmans, 2006), 496–8.

3–4. Bethany is located in the West Bank area of Palestine.

5–16. Julie M. Smith notes that the anointing woman's actions were prophetic, an indication of insight into Jesus' future, and furthermore that annointings are often done by prophets. See "She Hath Wrought a Good Work: The Anointing of Jesus in Mark's Gospel," *Studies in the Bible and Antiquity* 5 (2014) 31–46.

22. John's version of the annointing woman (John 12:1–8) is the only gospel that names the woman, this time as Mary, sister of Martha and Lazarus. See Mary Rose D'Angelo, "Woman Who Anoints Jesus," in *Women in Scripture: A Dictionary of Named and Unnamed Women in the Hebrew Bible, the Apocryphal/Deuterocanonical Books, and the New Testament*, eds. Carol Meyers, Toni Craven, and Ross S. Kraemer (Boston: Houghton Mifflin, 2000), 440–1.

Sapphira (The woman accused of fraud)

See Acts 5:1–11.

Joanna (Wife of Herod's chief of staff)

See Luke 8:1–3, 24:1–11.

5. Luke 24:11.

15. "One of the most radical things you can do is to actually believe women when they tell you about their experiences," Anita Sarkeesian, remarks at XOXO Festival, September 13, 2014, Portland, Oregon. For full presentation, see http://www.youtube.com/watch?v=ah8mhDW6Shs.

End Notes

Shoshan (Susanna)

See Luke 8:1–3.

The Hebrew form of the name Susanna (in Luke 8:3) is Shoshanna (שׁוֹשַׁנָּה), derived from the word *shoshan* (שׁוֹשָׁן). See Jeremy Corley, "Arboreal Metaphors and Botanical Symbolism in the Theodotion Susanna Narrative," in *The Metaphorical Use of Language in Deuterocanonical and Cognate Literature*, eds. Markus Witte and Sven Behnke (Berlin: De Gruyter, 2015), 129.

1. Adrian Hastings proposes that women who went to Jesus tomb, (such as Joanna and Susanna) were uncredited sources for Luke's gospel in *Prophet and Witness in Jerusalem: A Study of the Teachings of Saint Luke* (London: Longmans, Green, 1958), 38.

2–3. The destruction of the library at the ancient city of Alexandria in Egypt is often attributed to a single event, namely the conquest of Julius Caesar in 48 BC, however, scholars can point to a longer process of destruction due to multiple invasions throughout the centuries that followed. See Jean-Yves Empereur, "The Destruction of the Library of Alexandria: An Archaeological Viewpoint" in *What Happened to the Ancient Library of Alexandria?*, eds. Mostafa El-Abbadi and Omnia Mounir Fathallah (Leiden: Brill, 2008), 75–88.

4. One possible meaning for the name Shoshan is "lotus." See Corley, "Arboreal Metaphors and Botanical Symbolism in the Theodotion Susanna Narrative," 129.

5. Another meaning for Shoshan is "lily." See Corley, "Arboreal Metaphors and Botanical Symbolism in the Theodotion Susanna Narrative," 129.

7. Alternatively, Shoshan could mean "rose." See John Kitto, *A Cyclopedia of Biblical Literature: Vol III*, ed. William Lindsay Alexander (Philadelphia: J. B. Lippincott and Co, 1865), 844–5.

Damaris (An Athenian)

See Acts 17:22–34.

3. Areopagos (Ἀρείου Πάγου) is the hill in Athens where Paul preached in Acts 17:22–34 (NIV).

7. While there is a close linguistic connection to the word *damar* (δάμαρ) which can mean "wife," the name Damaris (Δάμαρις) may be derived from

the related word *damazo* (δαμάζω) which means "gentle," "subdued," or "tamed." See William Veitch, *Greek Verbs, Irregular and Defective. Their Forms, Meaning and Quantity*, (London: Clarendon, 1871), 145.

15. Areopagos is the "hill of Ares," named after the Greek god of war. It is also referred to as "Mars Hill," using the Roman name for Ares.

16. In the Greek pantheon, Athena, goddess of wisdom was also a deity associated with war.

20–22. Damaris might be altered from the name Damasandra (Δαμασάνδρα), which has a contrary meaning.

29. Hellas (Ελλάς) is the name for Greece in Hellenistic Greek.

33–35. Nothing is mentioned of Damaris in scripture besides her name.

38. Damasandra means "subduer of men."

Rhoda (A slave)

See Acts 12:12–17.

1–2. Acts 12:15.

4. Acts 12:16. Richard I. Pervo submits that this may poetic justice from a slave girl for Peter who lied to another slave girl when he denied Christ (Luke 22:56) in "Rhoda," in *Women in Scripture: A Dictionary of Named and Unnamed Women in the Hebrew Bible, the Apocryphal/Deuterocanonical Books, and the New Testament*, eds. Carol Meyers, Toni Craven, and Ross S. Kraemer (Boston: Houghton Mifflin, 2000), 145.

8. The name Rhoda (Ρόδη) means "rose" in Greek. See "Rhoda," http://biblehub.com/greek/4498.htm.

10–11. Acts 12:16–17.

Tabitha (A disciple)

See Acts 9:36–42.

1–3. Acts 9:36, Tabitha is specifically mentioned as a female disciple/pupil. See Lucinda A. Brown, "Tabitha," in *Women in Scripture: A Dictionary of Named and Unnamed Women in the Hebrew Bible, the Apocryphal/*

END NOTES

Deuterocanonical Books, and the New Testament, eds. Carol Meyers, Toni Craven, and Ross S. Kraemer (Boston: Houghton Mifflin, 2000), 159–60.

4. Acts 9:37.

5–6. Acts 9:36.

7–9. Acts 9:39.

10. Acts 9:40, Tabitha's name means "gazelle". See Brown, "Tabitha," 159.

Laishah & Eunike (The grandmother and mother of Timothy)

See 2 Tim 1:5.

The name of Timothy's grandmother's here is "Laishah," with sounds similar to Lois. See John F. A. Sawyer, *Isaiah* (Philadelphia: Westminster, 1984), 118. Her daughter Eunice's name is Hellenized as "Eunike" (Εὐνίκη). See Dorothy Kelley Patterson and Rhonda Kelley, eds. *Women's Evangelical Commentary, New Testament* (Nashville, TN: Broadman & Holman, 2006), 696.

1. 1 Cor 14:34, also written by Paul.

5. Prov 22:6 (ESV).

9–10. Luke 19:40.

12. Eunike/Eunice means "great victory."

13. Laishah, "lioness," is a feminine adaptation of a masculine word for lion, *layish* (לַיִשׁ).

17. Timothy owes his faith and ministry to his mother and grandmother, commended in a single verse.

Mariam al-Majdal (Mary Magdalene)

See Matt 27:55–61, 28:1–10; Mark 15:40–47, 16:1–11; Luke 8:1–3, 24:1–11; John 19:25, 20:1–18.

1. An Arabic name for Magdala, the seaside village north of Tiberias is Qaryat al-Majdal (قرية المجدل).

2. St. Ambrose recognized Mary Magdalene as *apostolorum apostola*, "Apostle to the Apostles." See Carolyn Dinshaw and David Wallace, *The*

End Notes

Cambridge Companion to Medieval Women's Writing (Cambridge, UK: Cambridge University Press, 2003), 2.

3. Al-Jalīl (الجليل) is the Arabic name for Galilee.

4. Various attempts have been made since the creation of the state of Israel to Judaize the Palestinian-majority area of Galilee.

5. Mark 16:9.

7–9. Mary Magdalene is often conflated with the unnamed "sinful" woman who anoints Jesus' feet in Luke 7:36–50.

12–16. John 20:11–18.

Prisca (Priscilla)

See Acts 18:2–3, 18–19, 24–26; Rom 16:3–5; 1 Cor 16:19; 2 Tim 4:19.

In the Greek, the name Prisca (Πρίσκα) is used in 2 Tim (in some versions additionally Rom and 1 Cor). "Priscilla" (Πρίσκιλλα) is the diminutive of this name. See Dominika A. Kurek-Chomycz, "Is There an 'Anti-Priscan' Tendency in the Manuscripts? Some Textual Problems with Prisca and Aquila," *Journal of Biblical Literature* 125 (2006) 107–28.

7. Prisca might mean "ancient." See Lockyer, *All the Women of the Bible*, 122.

8–9. In a 4:2 ratio, instances where the couple Prisca/Priscilla and her husband Aquila are named, Priscilla's name is first.

Phoebe (A deacon)

See Rom 16:1–2.

1–3. The name Phoebe (Φοίβη) means "radiant" and "bright." See Patterson and Kelley, *Women's Evangelical Commentary New Testament*, 407. Another interpretation is "pure or radiant as the moon." See Lockyer, *All the Women of the Bible*, 120.

4. Colin G. Kruse suggests that Phoebe could have been the courier of Paul's letter to the Romans in *Paul's Letter to the Romans* (Grand Rapids, MI: Eerdmans, 2012), 553.

5. Rom 16:1 "I commend to you our sister Phoebe, a deacon (*diakonos*) of the church in Cenchreae" (NIV).

6–9. Kruse, *Paul's Letter to the Romans*, 553.

10. Rom 16:4. See also Robert Jewett and Roy David Kotansky, *Romans: A Commentary*, ed. Eldon Jay Epp, (Minneapolis: Fortress, 2007), 90.

13–15. Rom 16:2.

Ilisabaʿ (Elizabeth)

See Luke 1:5–80.

Ilisabaʿ is a variation on the Arabic form of the name Elizabeth (إليشبع), noting the modern-day West Bank location of the Biblical couple, Elizabeth and Zacharias.

1. Luke 1:5 mentions Herod; Maltháki (Μαλθάκη) was one of Herod's wives at the time of John the Baptist's birth. See Tal Ilan, "Herodian Woman," *Jewish Women: A Comprehensive Historical Encyclopedia*, March 1, 2009, http://jwa.org/encyclopedia/article/herodian-women.

2. Yahuda (يهودا) is the Arabic name for Judea.

4. Al-Khalīl (الخليل) is the Arabic name for Hebron.

5. Harun (هارون) is the Arabic name for Aaron.

7–8. Luke 1:6.

9–13. Luke 1:7.

14–17. Luke 1:8–9.

18–19. Luke 1:11.

20–21. Luke 1:19.

22–25. Luke 1:13.

28. Ps 37:4.

Candace (Queen of Ethiopia)

See Acts 8:26–40.

1. Acts 8:26.

End Notes

2. Acts 8:27.

4. Acts 8:28.

8–9. Acts 8:27.

20. "Kandake" was not a name, but rather an Ethiopian title for the queen. See Richard Andrew Lobban, *Historical Dictionary of Ancient and Medieval Nubia* (Lanham, MD: Scarecrow, 2004), 97.

21–22. Acts 8:31.

23. Acts 8:28.

26. Acts 8:30.

33–35. Acts 8:31.

37. Acts 8:26.

49. Acts 8:36.

50–51. Acts 8:38.

55–56. Acts 8:39.

59. Ibid.

Bracha (The woman who blessed the mother of Jesus)

See Luke 11:27–28.

The Hebrew word *bracha* (בְּרָכָה) means "blessing."

1–10. Luke 11:27.

11–13. Luke 11:28, see also Mary Rose D'Angelo, "Women in Luke-Acts: a redactional view," *Journal of Biblical Literature* 109 (1990): 441–61.

14. See Vasiliki Limberis, "Woman Who Praises the Womb and Breasts of Jesus' Mother," in *Women in Scripture: A Dictionary of Named and Unnamed Women in the Hebrew Bible, the Apocryphal/Deuterocanonical Books, and the New Testament*, eds. Carol Meyers, Toni Craven, and Ross S. Kraemer (Boston: Houghton Mifflin, 2000), 444–5.

15–17. Luke 23:29; Gospel of Thomas 79.

18–19. Gen 27:29b (NIV).

End Notes

The "Other" Mary (One of many)

See Matt 27:61, 28:1.

42. The letters *mu* (μ), *mem* (מ), and *mīm* (م) represent the bilabial consonant "m" sound in Greek, Hebrew, and Arabic respectively.

44. The letters *resh* (ר) and *raa* (ر) represent an "r" sound in Hebrew and Arabic.

45. *Theta* (θ) represents the voiceless dental fricative "th" sound in Greek.

46. *Thaa* (ث) represents the voiceless dental fricative "th" sound in Arabic.

Kyria (Beloved lady of Second John)

See 2 John 1:1, 5.

Kyria (Κυρία) is the name or word John uses in the address of the letter, meaning noble or esteemed lady. Kyria is a well-documented personal name during the time of the epistle. See Ross S. Kraemer, "Elect Lady," in *Women in Scripture: A Dictionary of Named and Unnamed Women in the Hebrew Bible, the Apocryphal/Deuterocanonical Books, and the New Testament*, eds. Carol Meyers, Toni Craven, and Ross S. Kraemer (Boston: Houghton Mifflin, 2000), 500–1.

1. 2 John 1:1.

2. The letter was probably written to a church in Asia Minor, modern Turkey, possibly the church at Ephesus, (Turkish: *Efes*). See Kraemer, "Elect Lady," 500.

3. *Hanımefendi* is a feminine title of respect in Turkish.

9–10. Selçuk is a district of modern Turkey near where Ephesus is located; İzmir is the name of its province.

11. 2 John 1:8.

14–17. 2 John 1:12.

18. 2 John 1:2.

19. 2 John 1:12.

20–21. 2 John 1:3.

23–24. 2 John 1:13.

End Notes

Martha (Sister of Mary and Lazarus)

See Luke 10:38–42; John 11:1–39, 12:2.

1. In Luke 10:40, the many "tasks" over which Martha is troubled while Jesus is visiting are *diakonía* (διακονία), which is related to the word used in other references for deacon. See Mary Rose D'Angelo, "Martha," in *Women in Scripture: A Dictionary of Named and Unnamed Women in the Hebrew Bible, the Apocryphal/Deuterocanonical Books, and the New Testament*, eds. Carol Meyers, Toni Craven, and Ross S. Kraemer (Boston: Houghton Mifflin, 2000), 114–6.

2. A. T. Robertson notes that the Greek word *diákonos* (διάκονος) "properly means 'to kick up dust,' as one running an errand." "Diaconate" and "deacon" are derived from *diákonos*. See http://biblehub.com/greek/1249.htm.

10. Luke 10:39.

11–14. Luke 10:40.

19. Ibid.

21–24. In years of reading Martha's story, it had never occurred to the author that there was an alternative solution to Martha's complaint to Jesus. Rev. Betsy Johns Roadman presents another way in her sermon on the passage. See sermon delivered on July 22, 2007, St. Augustine's Church, Croton-on-Hudson, New York, Text: Luke 10:38–42, http://users.bestweb.net/~august/sermon22jul07.pdf.

Tryphaena & Tryphosa (God's workers)

See Rom 16:12.

1–2. Rom 16:12.

3–4. The names of both Tryphaena (Τρύφαινα) and Tryphosa (Τρυφῶσα) may derive from the same root *tryphaō* (τρυφάω), meaning "delicate" or "luxurious." See Mary Rose D'Angelo, "Tryphaena," in *Women in Scripture: A Dictionary of Named and Unnamed Women in the Hebrew Bible, the Apocryphal/Deuterocanonical Books, and the New Testament*, eds. Carol Meyers, Toni Craven, and Ross S. Kraemer (Boston: Houghton Mifflin, 2000), 165; Mary Rose D'Angelo, "Tryphosa," in *Women in Scripture: A Dictionary of Named and Unnamed Women in the Hebrew Bible, the Apocryphal/*

End Notes

Deuterocanonical Books, and the New Testament, eds. Carol Meyers, Toni Craven, and Ross S. Kraemer (Boston: Houghton Mifflin, 2000), 166.

5–6. The end of Tryphosa's name bears a link to the word *thoosa* (θόωσα), meaning "swift" or "nimble," which is also the name of a "water-nymph goddess of *swift currents*" in Greek mythology. See Robert A. Williams, *Savage Anxieties: The Invention of Western Civilization* (New York: Palgrave Macmillan, 2012), 27.

7. A Hebrew name of similar meaning to that of Tryphaena and Tryphosa is "Eden" (עֵדֶן) meaning, "delight." See Beverly Bow, "Edna," in *Women in Scripture: A Dictionary of Named and Unnamed Women in the Hebrew Bible, the Apocryphal/Deuterocanonical Books, and the New Testament*, eds. Carol Meyers, Toni Craven, and Ross S. Kraemer (Boston: Houghton Mifflin, 2000), 72.

8–11. Tryphaena may be Antonia Tryphaena, queen of Thrace, discipled by Thecla, according to the apocryphal *Acts of Paul and Thecla*. See Amy-Jill Levine and Maria Mayo Robbins, eds. *A Feminist Companion to the New Testament Apocrypha* (London: T & T Clark International, 2006), 146–205.

Lysia (A sister of Jesus)

See Matt 12:46, 13:53–58.

1. Luke 4:22.

2. John 5:24.

3. Matt 13:57; Mark 6:4; John 4:44.

6. Mark 3:31–35, 6:3–4; Luke 8:19–21.

8–12. The Coptic History of Joseph lists two of Jesus' sisters as Lydia and Lysia; other sources list Mary, Salome, and Anna. See Bart Ehrman and Zlatko Pleše, *The Apocryphal Gospels: Texts and Translations* (New York: Oxford University Press, 2011), 165; Richard Bauckham, *Gospel Women: Studies of the Named Women in the Gospels* (Grand Rapids, MI: W.B. Eerdmans, 2002), 231–3; and Frank Williams, *The Panarion of Epiphanius of Salamis, Books II and III. De Fide* (Leiden: Brill, 2012), 623.

17. Gen 37:7.

19. Gen 37:5.

22. Matt 6:10.

Chloe (A leader of the church in Corinth)

See 1 Cor 1:11.

2–3. 1 Cor 1:1.

6. 1 Cor 1:3.

7–9. 1 Cor 1:10.

13–15. 1 Cor 11:5–6.

16–18. 1 Cor 14:34–35.

19–21. 1 Cor 11:5–15; 1 Tim 2:9.

22. The capital of ancient Galatia was Ancyra, the site of Ankara, Turkey.

23–24. Gal 3:28.

25. Some scholars suggest the Galatian church were ethnic Celts. See Calvin J. Roetzel, *The Letters of Paul: Conversations in Context* (Louisville, KY: Westminster John Knox, 2015), 122–3.

26. Gal 3:28.

29. 1 Cor 11:5–6.

30. 1 Cor 14:34–35.

32–33. 1 Cor 7:7.

34. 1 Cor 15:58.

35. 1 Cor 16:13; 1 Tim 5:21.

36. 1 Tim 6:11.

www.ingramcontent.com/pod-product-compliance
Lightning Source LLC
Chambersburg PA
CBHW071430160426
43195CB00013B/1860